Big Fun Christmas Crafts & Activities

Over 200 Quick & Easy Activities for Holiday Fun!

by Judy Press

✵✵✵✵✵✵✵✵✵✵✵

illustrated by Sarah Cole

WILLIAMSON BOOKS
NASHVILLE, TENNESSEE

Dedication

To peace on earth

Text copyright © 2006 by Judy Press
Art copyright © 2006 by Ideals Publications

Library of Congress Cataloging-in-Publication Data

Press, Judy, 1944-
    Big fun Christmas crafts and activities : over 200 quick & easy activities
for holiday fun!   / by Judy Press;
    Illustrated by Sarah Cole.
        p. cm.
    Includes bibliographical references and index.
    ISBN 0-8249-6787-9 (casebound : alk. paper) — ISBN 0-8249-6786-0
(pbk. : alk. paper)
    1. Christmas decorations—Juvenile literature. 2. Handicraft—Juvenile
literature.   I. Cole, Sarah. II. Title.
TT900.C4.P755 2006
745.594'12—dc22

                                                    2006011394

Little Hands® series editor: **Susan Williamson**
Editor: **Michelle Peters**
Illustrations: **Sarah Cole**
Design: **Sydney Wright**
Cover design and illustrations: **Michael Kline**

Published by Williamson Books
An imprint of Ideals Publications
535 Metroplex Drive, Suite 250
Nashville, TN 37211
(800) 586-2572

Kids Can!®, *Little Hands*®, *Quick Starts for Kids!*®, *Kaleidoscope Kids*®, and *Tales Alive!*®
are registered trademarks of Ideals Publications, a division of Guideposts

Good Times™, Little Hands *Story Corners*™, and *Little Hands Kids Say …*™
are trademarks of Ideals Publications, a division of Guideposts

Permission to use the photographs on the following pages is granted by the author, Judy Press, to Ideals Publications: pages 32, 33, 44; permission to use the recipe No-Cook Kabobs from *Kids Cook! Fabulous Food for the Whole Family* on page 55 is granted by the authors, Sarah Williamson and Zachary Williamson.

Contents

Family & Friends – and So Much Fun!

It's Christmastime! Family and friends are gathering together to celebrate the season. Gifts are wrapped and hidden away, sweet and spicy aromas are coming from the kitchen, decorations have been hung, holiday music is being hummed and sung everywhere, and happy greetings are exchanged between friends and strangers alike. People are scurrying about, whispering excitedly, and genuinely enjoying this time of celebration.

Children are sure to get caught up in the merriment and more often than not, the excitement becomes overwhelming the closer we get to the holiday. Now is a wonderful time to use art and simple activities as a way to channel energy and vivid imaginations toward creative expression.

Big Fun Christmas Crafts & Activities is intended to help you and your little ones celebrate the season through crafts, games, friendship, read-aloud story times, and

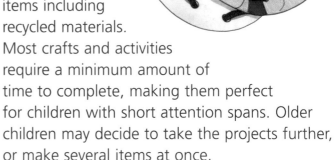

expressions of caring about others. Almost everything suggested can be made or accomplished with little effort, basic art supplies, and using household items including recycled materials. Most crafts and activities require a minimum amount of time to complete, making them perfect for children with short attention spans. Older children may decide to take the projects further, or make several items at once.

A Special Time for You and the Children!

These craft projects are intended to be open-ended, so the how-to instructions should be viewed as general guidelines, allowing for plenty of freedom of expression. Let originality, as well as the child's imagination and spontaneity, determine the outcome of any craft. Finished crafts need not hold any relation to what is suggested in the book, and to that end, avoid holding up finished projects as prototypes. Instead, every child will look at the supplies on the table, listen to the "name" of the project, and then proceed to craft totally imaginative pieces, enjoying the process as well as the end result.

Choices, Ideas & Suggestions to Ease Your Day!

If you're pressed for time or are leading a group of children, look for the QUICK & EASY sections, designed to provide a slightly less complicated, but similar version of the original craft. Use WAITING GAMES to engage in related activities that use other skills. AN ACT OF KINDNESS suggests ways to move children from the "me" of holiday time to focusing on others. Children are amazingly responsive to caring for and giving to others, and most of these suggestions take very little adult time to oversee.

Read aloud the books suggested in the LITTLE HANDS STORY CORNER™ sections to add other views and experiences to what the child knows. You'll find that Christmastime is a wonderful opportunity to read to older children, too. They will love hearing their favorite stories being read aloud, and they are not above squeezing into a chair or sofa, and joining in the coziness of listening to stories. This is a good time for older children to share their memories with younger ones, teaching them by example that shared experiences bring joy long after the event.

Help Children Celebrate Together!

In LIGHT UP THE NIGHT! (see pages 104–124), children focus on other holidays that occur in winter, such as Kwanzaa, Diwali, Hanukkah, and Chinese New Year. Encourage children to discuss their favorite holiday traditions with their friends and classmates from other cultural and religious backgrounds, while inviting all children to feel welcome in your own celebrations. If possible, share some of the foods and songs from different cultures, so

that children begin to see similarities and also begin to feel comfortable with differences.

Family, neighborhood, and school traditions and celebrations throughout the year provide a sense of security in a world that often moves too fast for little ones. Spending time with a child to create a special gift, hang a homemade decoration, surprise a neighbor, or make a greeting card is a wonderful way to keep the focus on what's important in your life and to welcome others into your home and community.

One of the best gifts of any holiday is the family time and friend time you spend together, sharing, loving, and giving. I hope the ideas in this book will remind you of some old traditions you want to start again or give you some fresh new ideas to try. May there be love and peace each day of the New Year. From my home to yours, from one classroom to another, I wish you a most joyful holiday!

Judy Press

Safety First!

In order to provide a safe environment for creativity, keep child safety in mind from the planning stages until the crafting supplies are put away.

Always work in a well-ventilated room, especially when using permanent markers, and glues or sprays. This means cracking the windows open and opening interior doors.

Always use child-safety scissors, which are much improved over the ones we all used as children. Teach children how to walk with scissors and how to hand them to another person. In activities where there are adult scissors or other adult-only sharp objects, be sure to keep them out of reach of all children.

Avoid choking hazards by controlling the supply of small items that younger children may grab and put in their mouths, such as beads, dried beans, rice, macaroni, hard candy, toothpicks, and confetti. Rather than putting small items on the table, keep a supply in your pocket and give each child only what is needed, when it is needed.

Small objects such as toothpicks and plastic or wooden skewers are sharp, so limit their use to times when you are working with one to three children, rather than larger groups.

Do not use glitter with young children. Glitter left on a child's hands can cause eye abrasions, if the child rubs her eyes.

Working on any of the activities in this book is centered on the fun and conviviality of the holiday season. If you model appropriate behaviors when using crafting tools and supplies, then children will follow your example and develop safe crafting practices, too.

Christmas Is A-Coming!

Cookies are in the oven,
The fire is burning bright.
Outside the snow is glistening
On this joyful winter's night.

Gathered all together,
Everyone is here.
It's time to start the holiday
With warm wishes and good cheer!

Hands-Together-Garland

❄ ❄

Hang this garland over a doorway,
along a fireplace mantel, or on a Christmas tree.
Put a three-person garland on
a special gift package anytime of year.

What you need:

❊ 5 or more Popsicle or craft sticks (wide ones)

❊ Markers, assorted colors

❊ Yarn, about 4 feet (120 cm) per Popsicle stick, assorted colors

❊ 5 pipe cleaners, assorted colors

Note: To make a longer garland, just double — or even triple — the amount of each material you use.

What you do:

1. To make your Popsicle stick people, draw a face and some hair on one end of each stick, and pants and shoes on the other end. Make each person different.

2. Wrap the yarn around each Popsicle stick to cover the middle section for a shirt.

3. Wrap a pipe cleaner around each stick for hands and arms. Twist pipe-cleaner "hands" with Popsicle-stick "neighbor" to link the people.

An Act of Kindness
Ask everyone to sign her handprint (see MAKE A HANDPRINT WREATH, this page). Then write "Merry Christmas" on the top center handprint. Ask a grown-up to help you hang it on a neighbor's door.

QUICK & EASY

Make a Handprint Wreath: Trace the handprints of each person in your family or classroom onto construction paper. Ask a grown-up to help you cut out the hand shapes and glue them together in a big wreath shape. If you have pets, don't forget their paw prints!

The Most Famous Reindeer of All

What you need:

* ❄ 2 brown paper lunch bags
* ❄ Child-safety scissors
* ❄ 2 brown pipe cleaners
* ❄ White glue
* ❄ Red pom-pom or red marker
* ❄ Black marker

What you do:

1. Open one of the paper bags and lay it flat. Cut out a triangle for the reindeer's head. Draw the reindeer's ears and cut out the shapes.

2. Bend the pipe cleaners into antlers. Glue the antlers, ears, and head onto the flap of the second bag.

3. Glue on the pom-pom for the reindeer's nose, or draw the nose with red marker. Draw on the reindeer's eyes with the black marker.

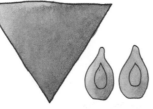

WAITING GAMES

Put on a Rudolph Face! To make antlers, trace your hands (with fingers outspread) onto two sheets of brown construction paper and cut out. Tape the shapes onto a band of construction paper that fits around your head. Use face paint to make a red nose and sing "Rudolph, the Red-Nosed Reindeer."

An Act of Kindness

Though you probably don't have a pet reindeer like some *Nenet* children in Russia do, I'm guessing that you like to play with your pets. Toss a ball for your dog to fetch or dangle some yarn for your cat. Animals like to play, too, just like you! (Before you play, ask a grown-up for permission, and please don't play with any animals that aren't yours. Thank you.)

Customs Around the World

He-r-r-re Rudi, Rudi, Rudi!

Do you know the story about Rudolph? From the beginning to the end? Have you ever seen a live reindeer? Well, most of us haven't, but the children who live in the Arctic regions of Europe and Asia know all about reindeer. They depend on reindeer for food, clothing, and shelter. What's the most unusual kind of animal that you have ever seen?

YUMMY TREATS

Tuna-Salad Reindeer

1 can of tuna, drained
Mayonnaise
3 slices of whole-wheat bread,
cut in half to make triangles
6 seedless grapes
3 cherry tomatoes
6 pretzel twists

Materials: medium bowl; fork; knife (for grown-up use only)

Yield: 3 sandwiches with reindeer faces

Mix the tuna and mayonnaise in the bowl and spread it on the cut bread. Decorate each reindeer with grapes for eyes and a tomato for a nose. Use the pretzel twists for antlers.

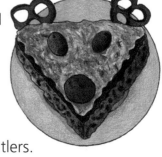

Candy-Cane Wreath

What you need:

* 3 red and 3 white pipe cleaners, cut in half
* Child-safety scissors
* 1 large white paper plate
* Green and red tempera paint, in separate jar lids
* Kitchen sponge
* Paintbrush
* Transparent tape
* Hole punch
* Ribbon or yarn

What you do:

1. Twist one red and one white pipe cleaner together, then bend them into a candy-cane shape. Repeat until you have used all of the pipe cleaners.

2. Ask a grown-up to help you cut out the center of the paper plate. Dab the sponge into the green paint. Press it onto the plate's rim in the shape of a wreath. Let dry.

3. Paint red berries on the wreath. Tape the candy canes around the wreath.

4. Thread ribbon or yarn through a hole punched in the top of the plate and hang up the wreath.

WAITING GAMES

Make a Holiday Place Mat: Cut out pictures from old magazines and cards (with permission). Or, draw pictures of candy canes and cut out. Glue the pictures onto construction paper and seal with clear contact paper. Set your holiday table with your place mat. Make enough for your whole family to use during the week before Christmas.

An Act of Kindness

Do you know an older person without children at home? Ask a grown-up to bring you to that person's home to hang a candy cane on the door. Won't that be a nice surprise?

QUICK & EASY

Twist red and white pipe cleaners together to make pretend candy canes. Tape a long ribbon or piece of yarn across a door or bookcase and hook the candy canes over it. (If they all slide together, then use clothespins to hold them in place.)

YUMMY TREATS

Candy-Cane Topping
1 regular-sized candy cane

Materials: 1 zipper-style plastic bag; wooden mallet or frying pan; small bowl; spoon

Yield: 2 servings of topping

Place the candy cane inside the bag and zip it closed. Use the wooden mallet or the bottom of a frying pan to pound the candy cane into tiny pieces. Pour the pieces of candy into the small bowl. Sprinkle over ice cream or frosted cakes, or mix into a mug of hot chocolate. Yum!

Ho-Ho-Ho Stocking

Don't forget your pet!

Hang your decorated stocking for your pet. Help out Santa by filling a puppy's stocking with dog biscuit treats, rawhide, or a can of used tennis balls. A kitten's stocking might hold a catnip mouse and a ball of yarn. How nice of you to think of your pets!

What you need:

- ❄ 1 large padded envelope, 12.5" x 18" (31 x 45 cm)
- ❄ Red tissue paper
- ❄ Transparent tape
- ❄ Scissors (for grown-up use only)
- ❄ Hole punch
- ❄ Yarn
- ❄ Cotton balls or batting
- ❄ White glue
- ❄ Decorations such as curling ribbon (optional)

1. Wrap the envelope in tissue paper and tape to hold in place.

2. Ask a grown-up to cut into one edge of the envelope to make a stocking shape, keeping the other edge uncut. Re-tape the tissue paper around the cut edges.

3. Punch holes about a half-inch (1 cm) from the stocking's edge. "Sew" with the yarn. Glue on cotton for trim. Decorate as you wish.

Cut out the shape of a stocking from two sheets of construction paper. Glue the edges of the stocking together; decorate with markers, and glue on cotton balls or batting.

 Customs Around the World

"... and the stockings were hung by the chimney with care ..."

Do you ever wonder why we hang stockings on Christmas Eve? The legend of the Christmas stocking is a story of three sisters whose father had no money to pay their *dowries* (a gift to their future husbands) so that they could marry. Saint Nicholas, having heard of the sisters' situation, tossed three small bags of gold toward their home. The bags fell down the chimney. The girls had hung their wet stockings by the fire to dry at night. And — you guessed it — the bags of coins landed (*plop!*) in the stockings! And that is how our custom is said to have begun.

Festive Ch❄❄-Ch❄❄ Train

What you need:

- ❄ 4 cardboard milk cartons,
  1 one-quart (1 L), 3 one-pint
  (500 ml), rinsed and dried
- ❄ Holiday wrapping paper, recycled,
  assorted patterns; or, brown paper
  bags (cut open so flat), decorated
  with markers

- ❄ Toilet-paper tube
- ❄ Aluminum foil, recycled
- ❄ Transparent tape
- ❄ Ribbon
- ❄ Black construction-paper scraps
- ❄ White glue

What you do:

1. Wrap each milk carton with the wrapping paper or decorated brown paper bag. Wrap the toilet-paper tube in the recycled aluminum foil.

2. Place the one-quart carton on its side. Tape a one-pint carton on one end and the toilet-paper tube in front to make the train's engine.

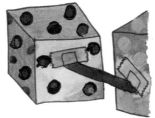

3. Use the ribbon and tape to attach the other two one-pint cartons to the back of the engine for train cars.

4. Cut out circles from the black construction paper for train wheels and glue them to the sides of the engine and cars.

An Act of Kindness

Ask a grown-up if you can wrap up some small toys that you are done using (see ALL WRAPPED UP!, pages 65–81). Fill your train's caboose with these tiny toys. When a friend visits, invite him to take one of the presents.

QUICK & EASY

Make a kid-sized train from two large cardboard boxes. Ask a grown-up to cut away the flaps. Draw a train engine on the first box, then fill the second box with toys. Attach the boxes together with string. Sit inside the engine and drive the train!

WAITING GAMES

Cut out words, greetings, and pictures from old holiday cards. See how many rebus* sentences you can make. Tape or glue the sentences on holiday-colored construction paper to create a story or poem.

* In a rebus, substitute a picture for a word, such as using a picture of a sled instead of writing s-l-e-d in the sentence.

Jolly Santa Puppet

What you need:

- ❄ Small white paper plates
- ❄ Red and black markers
- ❄ Child-safety scissors
- ❄ White glue
- ❄ 1 sheet of red construction paper, cut into strips 1½" x 8" (3.5 x 20 cm)
- ❄ Pencil
- ❄ Red and black construction-paper scraps
- ❄ Cotton balls or batting
- ❄ Transparent tape

What you do:

1. Draw Santa's suit on the back of one paper plate. Cut off the rim of the other plate by making a cut through the rim. Set aside the center circle. Cut through the rim again so that it is in two halves.

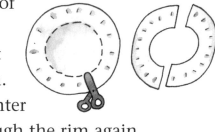

2. Draw Santa's face on the circle that you set aside and glue it onto Santa's suit to make Santa's head. Glue on the rim halves for Santa's beard.

3. Accordion-fold (see HOW TO ACCORDION-FOLD, this page) the four strips of red paper. Glue them onto the puppet for Santa's arms and legs.

4. Cut out Santa's mittens, boots, and hat from the black and red paper, and glue them on. Glue on the cotton balls for trim.

5. Tape a strip of paper onto the back of the puppet. Slide one hand under the paper strip to operate the puppet.

✐ How to Accordion-Fold ✐

Fold a strip of paper in half. Then, open the fold.

Bring both edges to the fold line in the center.

Reverse the center fold.

That's all there is to it!

YUMMY TREATS

Santa's Very Berry Shake

1 cup (250 ml) milk
1 cup (250 ml) fresh or frozen strawberries
1 cup (250 ml) plain yogurt

Materials: spoon; blender; spatula; 2 glasses
Yield: 2 glassfuls

Ask a grown-up to help you put all of the ingredients in a blender and whirl until smooth. Pour into two glasses.

LITTLE HANDS STORY CORNER™

McDuff's New Friend by Rosemary Wells
Little Hands Paper Plate Crafts by Laura Check
(a crafting book for ages 3 to 6)

QUICK & EASY

Draw Santa's face on a small white paper plate. Cut out a triangle from red construction paper. Glue the triangle onto the plate for Santa's hat. Glue on cotton balls for Santa's beard.

An Act of Kindness

Invite a friend or neighbor over to your home (with permission, of course,) to listen to a grown-up read aloud the poem "The Night Before Christmas" by Clement Moore. Afterward, talk about which part of the poem you each like best.

WAITING GAMES

Do a Family Jigsaw Puzzle: In the beginning of December, start working on a jigsaw puzzle with your family. Choose a spot to work on the puzzle where it won't be in the way, such as on a card table. Add a few puzzle pieces each night. See if you can complete the puzzle the night before you celebrate Christmas or a special holiday.

 ## Customs Around the World

How do you say Santa?

Children from around the world use different names for Santa Claus, also known as *Saint Nicholas* and *Saint Nick*. No matter what name they use, children wait excitedly — just like you — to see what treats he has left for them.

In Chinese: *Dun Che Lao Ren* (dwyn-chuh-lau-oh-run), or "Christmas Old Man"

In Italian: *Babbo Natale* (BAH-boh-na-tall-ee), or "Father Christmas"

In Japanese, *Santa no ojisan* (Santa-no-OH-gee-sahn), or "Uncle Santa"

In Dutch, *Sintirklaas* (SIN-ter-klaz), or "Saint Nicholas"

Which language's name sounds the most like the English language's Santa Claus?

Two Fir Trees

What you need:

- ❄ 2 sheets of green construction paper
- ❄ Child-safety scissors
- ❄ Pencil
- ❄ White tempera paint, in a jar lid and/or red and yellow tempera paint, in separate jar lids
- ❄ Kitchen sponge and/or 2 pencils with erasers
- ❄ Stapler

1. Cut the construction paper in half. Fold each half

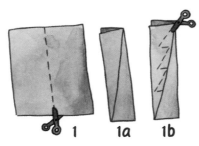

1   1a   1b

the long way. To make the tree shape, draw a line from the far corner on the bottom to the fold line on the top. Then, cut a jagged edge along that line.

2. For a snow-covered tree, dip the sponge in the white paint and dab onto the trees for snow. For a decorated Christmas tree, dip the eraser end of one pencil in the yellow paint and dab onto the trees. Repeat with the other pencil and the red paint.

3. Stack the snow-covered tree-pieces together. Ask a grown-up to help you staple them down the center.

Separate the "branches" so the tree stands upright. Repeat to make the decorated tree.

YUMMY TREATS

Holiday Veggie Tree
1 package of hard cheese,
such as Monterey Jack or cheddar
Assorted fresh vegetables: cherry tomatoes,
cauliflower and broccoli florets, cucumber slices,
and sliced green and red peppers

Materials: 1 green Styrofoam tree (from craft store), 12" (30 cm) tall

Yield: 1 veggie tree

Use toothpicks to attach the vegetables to the tree.

Note: You will know if your child can eat safely from a toothpick. The adult should control the toothpicks by giving out a few at a time, keeping the rest in a pocket and away from any nearby toddlers.

LITTLE HANDS STORY CORNER™

Mr. Willowby's Christmas Tree by Robert Barry

To make a tree stencil, ask a grown-up to help you cut out the shape of a tree from the center of a plastic deli lid. Place the stencil on light-colored paper and then dab on green tempera paint all

around and over the stencil. Lift the stencil to see the print. Now move the stencil and repeat until you have a small grouping of trees.

Customs Around the World

Oh, Christmas tree, Oh, Christmas tree ...

Some families in the United States and Canada live where they can walk into the woods to cut down a fresh Christmas tree. Then, they carry or pull it back on a sled to their car or truck. It is a lot of work, but when the tree is in the house it smells wonderful! Norwegian families go out into the woods to select their Christmas trees, too. Before the presents are opened, the family dances in a circle around the tree while singing traditional Christmas carols. How do you get your tree and what do you decorate it with?

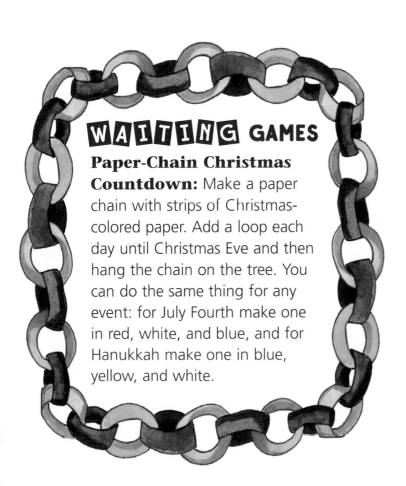

WAITING GAMES

Paper-Chain Christmas Countdown: Make a paper chain with strips of Christmas-colored paper. Add a loop each day until Christmas Eve and then hang the chain on the tree. You can do the same thing for any event: for July Fourth make one in red, white, and blue, and for Hanukkah make one in blue, yellow, and white.

An Act of Kindness
Share your holiday traditions with a good friend or neighbor. Ask a grown-up to invite a friend who doesn't celebrate Christmas to help decorate your tree. Then, when your friend has a special religious or cultural holiday, she can invite you to her house to participate in her traditions.

Christmas Cards & Happy Wishes

Christmas greetings in the mailbox
Are sent by people far and wide.
Here's a card from Gram and Grandpa,
Who live in the countryside.

There's news from friends and family,
And a surprise from Auntie Sue —
Tucked inside's a picture
Of her baby who's brand new!

Starry-Night Card

What you need:

* 1 sheet of blue cardstock,
  8½" x 11" (21 x 27.5 cm)
* Hole punch (or star punch)
* Aluminum foil scraps, recycled
* Glue stick
* 2 sheets of construction paper,
  1 black and 1 yellow

What you do:

1. Fold the cardstock in half. Hold the card the long way and punch holes or stars across the top so they look as if you sprinkled them on the card (rather than placing them in a straight line). Glue foil over the holes from the inside of the card.

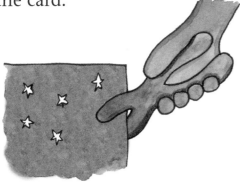

2. Cut out building shapes from the black construction paper. For a cityscape, cut out some tall buildings like sky-scrapers. For a countryscape, cut out houses and barns. Glue them onto the front of the card.

3. Cut out small window shapes from the yellow con-struction paper and glue them onto the buildings to look as if the lights are on inside.

WAITING GAMES

Stargazing Fun: On a cold, crisp night, ask a grown-up to take you outside for some winter stargazing. Try to find a spot where there aren't a lot of streetlights. Before you go outdoors, look at a book about stargazing or go to the Hayden Planetarium website (www.amnh.org/rose/haydenplanetarium.html) to see what some of the groups of stars, called constellations, look like. Notice the *Big Dipper* and *Little Dipper*. Then, bring along a thermos of hot Easy Christmas Cocoa (see page 27) and a sleeping bag or warm blanket. Lie down on your back and gaze up at the stars. Do you see any of the constellations? Do you see any shooting stars speeding by?

YUMMY TREATS

Easy Christmas Cocoa

1 cup (250 ml) milk per person
Cocoa mix, according to directions
Marshmallow fluff or mini marshmallows
Peppermint stick or candy cane

Materials: small pot or microwavable bowl; measuring spoons; measuring cup; thermos or mugs; zipper-style plastic bag

Yield: One mug per cup of milk

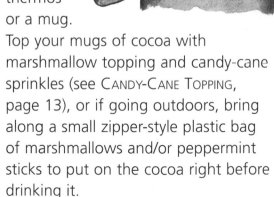

Ask a grown-up to help you heat the milk to a near boil on the stovetop or in the microwave. Add the hot milk to the cocoa in either a thermos or a mug.

Top your mugs of cocoa with marshmallow topping and candy-cane sprinkles (see CANDY-CANE TOPPING, page 13), or if going outdoors, bring along a small zipper-style plastic bag of marshmallows and/or peppermint sticks to put on the cocoa right before drinking it.

QUICK & EASY

For another starry card, fold a piece of blue cardstock in half. Draw a line about a third of the way down from the top to look as if it were a distant mountaintop. Cut out yellow, white, or silver stars in different sizes from construction paper and foil. Glue the stars to the card above the mountaintops.

 LITTLE HANDS STORY CORNER™

Zoo in the Sky by Jacqueline Mitton

Pop-Up New Year's Card

What you need:

- ❄ 2 sheets of cardstock, 8½" x 11" (21 x 27.5 cm), two colors
- ❄ Black marker
- ❄ Child-safety scissors
- ❄ Hole punch
- ❄ 2 strips of thin ribbon, each 3" (7.5 cm)
- ❄ White glue

What you do:

1. Draw two bells (or any other shape) on one sheet of cardstock and cut out the shapes. Cut out two strips, 2" x ³/₄" (5 x 2 cm) from the cardstock scraps. Fold the other sheet of cardstock in half for the card.

2. Punch a hole in the top of each bell. Thread ribbon through the hole and tie a bow on each bell.

3. To make the bells pop off the card, accordion-fold (see How to Accordion-Fold, page 19) the two strips of cardstock. Glue one end of one strip to the back of one bell and the other end to the front of the folded card. Repeat with the second strip and bell. See how they pop up?

Ring in the New Year with a noisemaker. Decorate a plastic container with holiday stickers or used wrapping paper. Fill the container with dried beans, rice, or macaroni. Place the lid on the container and give it a shake to ring in the New Year!

An Act of Kindness

A good deed, indeed! During school vacation, invite your siblings to clean out their closets and toy chests of the used books, games, and toys that you and your family are not using anymore. Stack them up and ask a grown-up to help you find a place to deliver them to children who might enjoy them. Then, make a card and write "Have fun!" inside.

𝕎𝔸𝕀𝕋𝕀ℕ𝔾 GAMES

Make a New Year's Wish Box: Write down your wishes for the coming year on slips of paper, sign your name, and add the date. Put the papers in a shoebox and put the box away. For added fun, cover the top and the bottom of the shoebox separately with SNOWY-DAY WRAPPING PAPER (see pages 65–67). Open the box of wishes on New Year's Eve of the following year to see if your wishes came true!

 ## Customs Around the World

Happy New Year!

New Year's Eve is celebrated in many different ways around the world. If you live in North America, on December 31st, you'll count down the last ten seconds before midnight: "… 5, 4, 3, 2, 1," then shout out, "Happy New Year!" as the clocks strike midnight.

In Spain, people pop a grape into their mouths on each of the 12 strokes of the clock at midnight. Twelve grapes mean good luck for each month of the upcoming year.

In Denmark, it's nice to find many broken dishes on your doorstep on New Year's Day. That's right. Broken dishes! At midnight, grown-ups break old dishes in their friends' doorways as a way to send Happy New Year wishes!

YUMMY TREATS

New Year's Eve Fizzy

1 6-ounce (180 ml) can frozen juice
concentrate (orange, apple, grape,
or pineapple), thawed
Carbonated water, chilled
4 orange slices
4 maraschino cherries

Materials: mixing bowl; wooden spoon;
fancy plastic glasses (if available);
4 plastic toothpicks (if age-appropriate)

Yield: 4 servings

In a mixing bowl, stir together the fruit
juice concentrate and three juice cans
of carbonated water. Pour into glasses
and garnish with an orange slice and
a cherry, skewered on a toothpick.

fizzy-licious!

Make a New Year's Resolution!

A New Year's resolution is a promise to yourself to try to change or improve a particular behavior that causes you problems. Do you forget to raise your hand in school before speaking? Do you put your fingers in your mouth? Do you forget to say "Please" and "Thank you"? Maybe you pick fights with your little brother or cause problems at dinnertime? Whatever it is, remember that it must be something you want to change about yourself, not something you wish other people would change.

Fold a piece of paper in half, as if you were making a card. Open it and lay it flat. On the first side, draw a big circle. Inside it, draw a picture of *what you would like to stop doing,* such as a picture of a girl with her fingers in her mouth. Then put a big line through it, which is the symbol for "No." Then, on the next

side, draw a picture of you behaving the way you would prefer, such as a picture of you, reading a book, without your fingers in your mouth. Each day look at the picture and ask yourself, "Did I follow my New Year's resolution today?"

Surprise! Greeting Card

What you need:

* 1 sheet of cardstock, 8½" x 11" (21 x 27.5 cm), any color
* Scissors for adult use only
* Markers, assorted colors
* Old photo (with permission)
* Transparent tape

1. Fold the cardstock in half and hold the card the long way. To make a double door, ask a grown-up to help you cut out three sides (top, bottom, and middle) without cutting into the bottom edge of  the card. The doorway should be slightly smaller than the photo.

2. Draw a house (the pointed roof and the sides) around the doorway. Tape the photo inside the card so it shows through the front of the card when you open the doors. Surprise!

Draw a house on the front of a piece of folded construction paper. Glue a photo of your family or pet in the doorway of the house.

WAITING GAMES

Paint a Window Holiday Scene: Gather tempera paints, clear dishwashing liquid, small containers for paint, paintbrushes, masking tape, newspaper, and paper towels. Spread the newspaper and tape the window sash. Mix powdered paint with dish soap until it's thick like sour cream or mix a small amount of dish soap with premixed paints. Using only a little paint on your paintbrush at a time, paint your scene. To make changes or erase, wipe paint away with a dry paper towel.

Stained-Glass Card

What you need:

- ❄ 1 sheet of black construction paper
- ❄ Child-safety scissors
- ❄ Small strips of tissue paper, assorted colors
- ❄ Glue stick
- ❄ 1 sheet of cardstock, 8¹/2" x 11" (21 x 27.5 cm), any color

What you do:

1. To make the window, cut out a rectangle or other window shape from the black construction paper. (It will need to fit on the front of the card.) Fold the black shape in half. Cut into the folded edge of the window along the fold lines, making small cutouts, as if you were making a snowflake.

2. Open the window flat. Glue small strips of different-colored tissue paper on the back of the window over the openings.

3. Fold the cardstock in half and glue the window onto the front.

QUICK & EASY

On a piece of folded cardstock, color the front of the card with brightly colored crayons, changing colors frequently and pressing hard. Then, cover your bright colors with a black crayon, pressing hard. Using the side of a Popsicle stick or craft stick, scrape off shapes of color, leaving the black lines between the color-stained sections — just like a stained-glass window!

 LITTLE HANDS STORY CORNER™

Dreamer from the Village: The Story of Marc Chagall
by Michelle Markel
(Marc Chagall is famous for his wonderful stained-glass windows, among other things.)

WAITING GAMES

Play Christmas Card Memory:
Cut the fronts of last year's cards in half and place them face-down. Take turns turning over two halves at a time. If the halves match, put them aside. If not, turn them back over for the next player. Continue playing until all the halves are matched.

Too easy? Cut cards in thirds and see if you can get three pieces to match, by turning over three pieces at a time! Wow! You sure are good at this!

YUMMY TREATS

Easy Stained-Glass Cookies

½ cup white cake frosting (homemade or store-bought)
Food coloring (three colors)
1 prebaked sugar cookie (homemade or store-bought)
1 tube cake-decorating gel, black

Materials: small bowls (3); spreading utensil

Yield: 1 stained-glass cookie

Divide the white frosting into thirds. Use a drop of food coloring to tint the frosting different colors for the "glass." Spread the frosting on the cookie with edges touching to make the blocks of color. Trace around the colors with the black decorating gel. Allow the frosting to dry.

Embossed-Foil Card

Happy Holidays!

Warm Wishes

What you need:

* ❄ 2 sheets of cardstock, 8¹/₂" x 11" (21 x 27.5 cm), any two colors
* ❄ Child-safety scissors
* ❄ White glue
* ❄ Aluminum foil, recycled
* ❄ Marker

What you do:

1. Fold both sheets of cardstock in half; set one aside to use as the card. Using the other folded piece of cardstock, cut out a fairly large rectangle from one half and a holiday shape (tree, bell, ornament, menorah, kinara, snowflake) that will fit inside the rectangle from the other half.

2. Glue the shape onto the rectangle. Wrap the rectangle in aluminum foil. Press around the raised shape. Draw around the holiday shape with a marker.

3. Glue the foil rectangle onto the front of the folded card. Now, write a greeting and your name inside.

QUICK & EASY

Make a String-Foil Card. Fold a piece of construction paper in half. Glue some pieces of yarn or heavy string onto the front of the card in designs or in Christmas shapes. Cover the card front with recycled aluminum foil and press around the string shapes. Glue down the corners of the foil. Draw around the shapes with a marker.

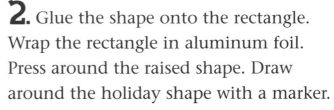
WAITING GAMES

Thank You, Mail Carrier!
Mike B. from Hershey, Pennsylvania, tells us, "Every holiday we give our mail carrier a special treat of home-baked cookies. She works really hard delivering our mail, especially at the holidays." We think that is a great idea, Mike. Maybe you would like to prepare CHRISTMAS TRAIL MIX (see page 39) for all your pick-up or delivery people, such as the newspaper deliverer and the trash pick-up person. Be sure to enclose a card that you make with the treats.

Christmas Trail Mix

This is so good that you might want to prepare
extra for special "thank you" gifts at Christmastime.

1 cup (250 ml) unsalted nuts
1 cup (250 ml) sunflower seeds
1 cup (250 ml) banana chips
1 cup (250 ml) chocolate chips
1 cup (250 ml) raisins
1 cup (250 ml) craisins

*Because of the danger of
allergic reactions to peanuts,
please do not add peanuts to the mix.

Materials: large bowl; dry measuring
cups; wooden spoon; zipper-style
plastic bags

Yield: 6 cups of mix

Mix together all of the ingredients in
the bowl. You can add or substitute
other ingredients. Pour a cup of the
trail mix into each zipper-style plastic
bag. Give as a "thank you" gift or
tuck a bag into a Christmas stocking.

 LITTLE HANDS STORY CORNER™

The Jolly Christmas Postman by Janet & Allan Ahlberg

Confetti-Ornament Card

✳ ✳ ✳

Season's Greetings!

What you need:

- ❄ 1 sheet of cardstock, 8½" x 11" (21 x 27.5 cm), any color
- ❄ Marker
- ❄ Scissors for adult use only
- ❄ Wrapping paper or construction-paper scraps
- ❄ Hole punch
- ❄ Contact paper
- ❄ Transparent tape

1. Fold the cardstock in half. Draw the shape of an ornament. Ask a grown-up to help you cut out the shape without cutting into the edges of the card.

2. Punch holes in the wrapping paper and save the dots. If you have some sparkling paper, use that too.

3. Cut two sheets of contact paper slightly larger than the ornament cutout. Peel back the paper from the first sheet and sprinkle the dots on the sticky side. Peel back paper from the second sheet and place it on top of the first sheet.

Make Colorful Confetti! Using a hole punch, punch out confetti dots from some used wrapping paper, foil, or newspaper comic pages. Fold a piece of cardstock in half and draw a big Christmas shape on the front. Working on a small space at a time, spread glue inside the shape and sprinkle your confetti on the glue. Gently press the confetti in, let dry, and send your card to a friend or relative with a holiday greeting!

4. Tape the contact paper inside the card to cover the ornament opening so you have a sparkling, bright confetti ornament showing through.

 LITTLE HANDS STORY CORNER™

A Happy New Year's Day by Roch Carrier

WAITING GAMES

Making Envelopes: Do you have a friend who moved away? Do you think of him sometimes and wonder what he is doing? Sending Christmas and New Year's cards is a nice way to let people know that you think about them throughout the year, even if you don't see them often. Here's how to make an envelope for mailing your card.

1. Place your folded greeting card in the center of a sheet of plain paper. Leave space on all sides to allow the card to slide in and out easily.

2. Fold the paper neatly around all four edges of the card.

3. Open the paper flat and cut away the four rectangular corners.

4. Then, cut the edges of the flaps on a slant, as shown.

5. Fold in the sides, then fold up the bottom of the paper and tape to hold.

Gifts to Make & Give

Little hands are busy,
With paper and with glue.
A very special present
Will come from me to you.

There's a place mat for the table
And a chime to hang outdoors,
Plus a frame and pencil holder
That can't be found in stores!

Magnetic Picture Frame

What you need:

* Clear plastic deli lid
* Pencil
* Old photo
  (with permission)
* Child-safety scissors
* White glue
* Ribbon
* Magnetic tape

step 1a

step 1b

What you do:

1. Trace around the deli lid on the back of the photo. Cut out the photo a little smaller than the tracing, and glue it inside the lid.

2. Glue ribbon around the rim of the deli lid. Attach the magnetic tape to the back of the lid. Display the photo on a refrigerator door or other metal surface.

QUICK **&** EASY

Using the same techniques as in MAGNETIC PICTURE FRAME, Step 1 (see above), glue in either a photo or a holiday picture from an old card or magazine. Then, punch a hole in the top of the lid and thread a ribbon or piece of yarn through the hole. Give it to a friend as a Christmas present or hang up your ornament by the fireplace or in your room.

WAITING GAMES

Make a Holiday Treat Jar: Start with a large glass jar. Each day before the holiday, add a layer of dried fruits (raisins, craisins, apricots, or banana pieces) or nuts (no peanuts, please). If allowed, add a layer of chocolate or carob chips and one of jellybeans, too. Once the jar is filled, share the treat while you make crafts, play games, and listen to stories on the evenings leading up to Christmas Eve. Or, put a ribbon on the top and give it as a gift.

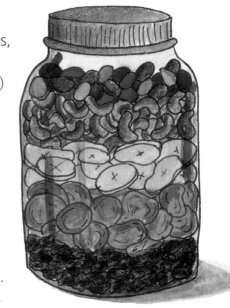

Hang Your Holiday Cards: Decorate clip-type clothespins with markers. Use the clothespins to hang Christmas cards on ribbon stretched from one wall to the other in a corner of a room. (You can do the same thing with birthday cards!)

Jingle-Bell Wind Chime

❄ ❄ ❄

What you need:

- ❅ Clear plastic water or soda bottle, ½ gallon (2 liters)
- ❅ Utility knife (for grown-up use only)
- ❅ Kitchen sponge
- ❅ Child-safety scissors
- ❅ White tempera paint, in a jar lid
- ❅ 4 strands of yarn, each 12" (30 cm) long, plus a strand to hang the wind chime, about 8" (20 cm) long
- ❅ 8 jingle bells

Note to adults: When working with young children and small items such as jingle bells, keep a supply in your pocket and give each child only what is needed. It is up to you to determine the suitability of working with small items around preschool children.

step 1

step 3

What you do:

1. Ask a grown-up to cut away three-fourths of the plastic bottle from the bottom. Ask a grown-up to poke four evenly spaced holes around the cut edge of the bottle.

2. Cut out the shape of a star from the sponge. Dip the sponge in the white paint and press it onto the bottle.

3. Thread the longer pieces of yarn through the holes in the bottle. Attach a single bell to each yarn end.

4. Tie the 8" (20 cm) piece of yarn around the neck of the bottle to hang the wind chime.

QUICK & EASY

Ask a grown-up to help you sew a jingle bell on each finger of an old glove. Now, put on the glove and shake your hand for a jingle-bell tune.

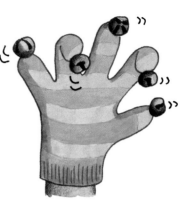

Little Hands Kids Say ...™

"We line up a few large drinking glasses and fill them with different amounts of water. Then, we take a spoon and tap on the glasses to make music," says Mandy S. from Solon, Ohio. "Everyone has to guess what holiday song we're playing."

An Act of Kindness

There's nothing quite as nice as a group of children caroling for the pleasure of others. Ask a grown-up to help you arrange to go caroling either around your neighborhood, at the entrance of a hospital, or at a senior citizen's center. Ask everyone to come with some bells on their mittens and then begin the carols by singing — you guessed it — "Jingle Bells!" Oh, what fun!

Stained-Glass Pencil Holder

What you need:

* Tissue paper scraps, assorted colors
* White glue, mixed with a few drops of water, in jar lid
* Paintbrush
* Clear plastic deli container, with lid
* Utility knife (for grown-up use only)
* Pens and pencils

What you do:

1. Tear the tissue paper into small pieces.

2. Use the paintbrush to brush the glue mixture around the outside of the deli container, a section at a time. Stick the pieces of tissue paper onto the container. The more pieces you stick on close together, the more colorful your pencil holder will appear.

3. Ask a grown-up to cut small X's in the lid of the container. Put the lid back on the container. Push pens and pencils through the X's.

WAITING GAMES

Make a Holiday Cardholder: Ask a grown-up to help you cut out a large Christmas-tree shape from a sheet of foam-core board (available at a craft or office supply store). Trace the tree onto a piece of green felt and cut out. Glue the felt onto the foam-core tree. Hang the tree on a wall with a peel-and-stick picture hanger. Use colorful pushpins to attach holiday greeting cards to the tree.

QUICK & EASY

Wrap an oatmeal container or other round, cardboard container in recycled Christmas wrapping paper or construction paper. Tie a ribbon around the middle of the container. Then fill it up with pencils and pens! What a nice, useful gift!

Peace Dove

What you need:

* Large white paper plate
* Child-safety scissors
* White tissue paper,
  6" x 14" (15 x 35 cm)
* Black marker
* Hole punch
* Yarn, about 8" (20 cm)

step 1

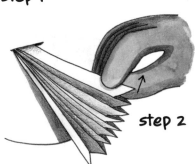

step 2

What you do:

1. Ask a grown-up to help you cut out the shape of a dove from the paper plate (see template below). Use the wavy edge of the plate for its tail feathers.

2. Accordion-fold (see HOW TO ACCORDION-FOLD, page 19) the tissue paper for wings. Cut a slit in the center of the dove. Slide the wings through the slit and open them slightly.

3. Draw on the dove's eyes. Punch a hole in the top of the dove's body and thread yarn through to hang it up.

Cut a white paper plate in half.
Cut one of the halves into three wedges. Glue one wedge onto the remaining plate half for a tail. Glue the other wedge onto the plate for the bird's head and beak. Glue on the third wedge for a wing.

TEMPLATE

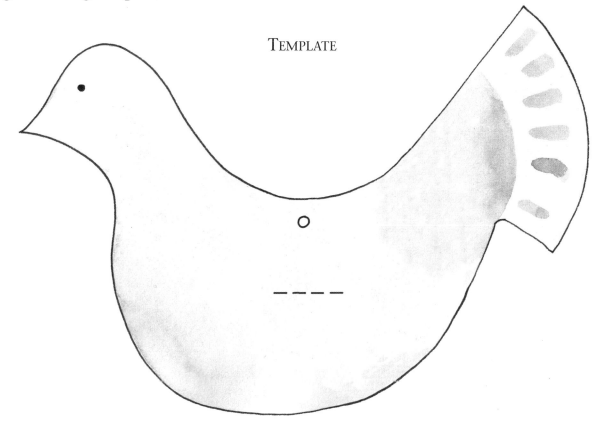

An Act of Kindness

Sometimes around Christmas or special days that everyone has been looking forward to for a long time, people have more disagreements than usual. When you have an argument with someone, is it hard to make up and say you are sorry? The strongest and bravest people know how to apologize and say that they are sorry. The next time you have a disagreement, try to do the right thing. Maybe it will be easier if you give your friend a PEACE DOVE (see page 50) when you say that you are sorry for what you said.

I know you can do it!

WAITING GAMES

Sing Your Own "The Twelve Days of Christmas": Replace the usual lyrics to the song with your own, such as, "one ball bouncing," "two friends singing," or "three ice-cream cones melting." Take turns adding items!

Five brownie sundaes!

Customs Around the World

The Dove of Peace

The dove is a symbol of love and peace. It is often shown on New Year's cards, as this is the time of year when people express their hopes for the coming year. And doves are drawn carrying an *olive branch*, which is another symbol of peace. Draw a picture of your feelings and ideas about peace, and hang it up for all to share.

LITTLE HANDS STORY CORNER™

Four Friends at Christmas by Tomie de Paola
Kids Care! by Rebecca Olien
(an activity book)

Picture-Perfect Place Mat

What you need:

- ❄ 1 sheet of white copy paper or construction paper
- ❄ Markers, assorted colors
- ❄ Waxed paper

- ❄ 2 sheets of newspaper
- ❄ Iron (for grown-up use only)
- ❄ Hole punch
- ❄ Yarn, about 4 feet (135 cm)

What you do:

1. Draw a holiday picture on the paper. Place the drawing in between two sheets of waxed paper that are slightly larger than the drawing.

2. Place the drawing and waxed paper between the two sheets of newspaper. Ask a grown-up to iron quickly back and forth over the newspaper to hold the waxed paper together.

3. Punch holes around the waxed paper. Thread yarn through the holes.

LITTLE HANDS STORY CORNER™

Emily's Art by Peter Catalanotto

QUICK & EASY

Trace a dinner plate, knife, fork, and spoon onto a sheet of construction paper. Cut fringe along the outer edges of the paper. When you set the table, use the place mat as a template.

WAITING GAMES

Set a Festive Holiday Table:
Fill a bowl with bright red cranberries, pinecones, or red and green apples. Place the bowl in the center of your table and surround it with boughs of evergreens.

No-Cook Kabobs

These colorful kabobs make a fun appetizer for your family's holiday meal or a nice snack when wrapping gifts. Be sure to eat them sitting down and keep the skewers pointing down, as you do with scissors.

Red and green apples
Red and green seedless grapes
Cheese of your choice, such as Swiss, cheddar, or mozzarella

Materials: knife (for grown-up use only); cutting board; plastic or wooden skewers (no metal); plate

Yield: as many as you like

Ask a grown-up to cut the apples and cheese into bite-sized pieces. Put the apple pieces, cheese pieces, and grapes onto a skewer in whatever order you like.

Note to adults: Please decide if your child is capable of using a skewer both in making and eating the kabobs. If in doubt, have the child arrange the fruit and cheese in a pattern on a plate, skipping the skewers completely.

No-Cook Kabobs adapted from *Kids Cook! Fabulous Food for the Whole Family* by Sarah Williamson & Zachary Williamson

Angel Tree-Topper

What you need:

* ❄ 1 uncooked egg in shell
* ❄ Pin or small nail
* ❄ 1 drinking straw
* ❄ Medium bowl
* ❄ Fine-point markers, assorted colors
* ❄ Large white paper plate
* ❄ Child-safety scissors
* ❄ Transparent tape
* ❄ 1 pipe cleaner
* ❄ 1 white coffee filter

What you do:

1. With a grown-up's help, carefully twist the pin into the pointed end of the egg to make a small hole. Then make another hole at the other end of the egg. (The holes should be wide enough for the straw and pipe cleaner to fit through them.)

2. Insert the straw into one of the holes and blow the egg white and yolk into the bowl, being careful not to get raw egg in your mouth.

3. Rinse the eggshell in water and let dry. (Wash your hands after handling raw eggs.) Gently draw on the angel's face and hair.

4. Cut the paper plate in half. Tape one half together for a cone shape. Draw the angel's arms and hands on the plate.

5. Ask a grown-up to help you insert the pipe cleaner through the holes in the egg. Leave about 4" (10 cm) of the pipe cleaner sticking out of the top of the egg and insert the rest through the top of the paper-plate cone. Tape the pipe cleaner inside the cone. Shape the top of the pipe cleaner into a halo and twist to secure.

6. Fold the coffee filter in half, then cut it in half for wings. Tape the wings onto the angel.

Drape a circle of white tissue paper over the top of a lollipop. Tie a ribbon under the candy ball for the angel's head. Wrap a pipe cleaner around the angel's head for a halo. Draw on the angel's face and hair. Fold a coffee filter in half, then cut it in half for wings. Tape the wings onto the angel.

An Act of Kindness

Isn't it fun to get mail addressed to you? Most everyone likes to get mail. If you have a classmate who seems to be sad, why not write her a note on a recycled card. Then, ask your teacher or another grown-up to help you address it to your friend. Won't she be surprised and happy when she receives it? That is a very nice thing to do!

 Little Hands Kids Say ...™

Turn Last Year's Holiday Cards into This Year's Thank-You Notes! That's what Brian and Eric S. from Queens, New York, tell us they do. This way they recycle and also get their thank-you notes written! First, fold a piece of construction paper into fourths. Then, glue a picture from one of the old cards onto the front of the new card. Ask a grown-up to help you write a thank-you greeting on a piece of white paper and glue it onto the inside of the card.

Note to adults: If children can't write yet, let them "dictate" what they want the note to say.

 LITTLE HANDS STORY CORNER™

Elijah's Angel: A Story for Chanukah and Christmas by Michael J. Rosen

Angels, Angels Everywhere by Tomie dePaola

Christmas Camel

What you need:

- Cardboard milk carton, 1 pint (500 ml), rinsed and dried
- Styrofoam or cardboard egg carton
- Child-safety scissors
- Transparent tape
- Brown paper lunch bag
- Black marker
- White glue
- 4 Popsicle or craft sticks
- Brown crayon

What you do:

1. Turn the milk carton on its side. Ask a grown-up to help you cut out two eggcups, still attached together, from the egg carton. Tape the two eggcups across the top side of the milk carton.

2. Open the paper bag and ask a grown-up to help you cut off the bottom. Lay the bag flat, then wrap it around the carton. Tape to secure.

3. Draw the camel's head, neck, and tail on the bottom of the bag, as shown (see template below). Cut out the shapes. Glue on the camel's head and neck, bending back the tab on the neck. Glue on the tail.

4. Color the Popsicle sticks brown. Ask a grown-up to cut four slits in the bottom of the milk carton. Insert the Popsicle sticks for the camel's legs.

TEMPLATE

FOLD

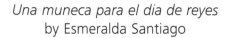

LITTLE HANDS STORY CORNER™

Una muneca para el dia de reyes
by Esmeralda Santiago

YUMMY TREATS

Mexican Hot Chocolate

Did you know that hot chocolate was first made
in Mexico many, many centuries ago? Imagine, it was
very popular then and it is still popular today!

2 cups (500 ml) milk
2 ounces (50 g) semisweet baking chocolate squares
2 ounces (50 g) milk chocolate squares or morsels
Ground cinnamon

Materials: saucepan; liquid measuring cup; wooden spoon;
wire whisk; 2 heatproof mugs

Yield: 2 mugs of hot chocolate

With a grown-up's help, pour the milk into the saucepan, place
the saucepan on the stove, and turn the heat on medium-high.
Break the chocolate squares into pieces and add them to the pot.
Stir constantly with the wooden spoon. As the chocolate melts,
turn the heat down to medium. Continue to stir until the chocolate
is completely melted. Ask a grown-up to whisk the chocolate milk
until it is foamy. Carefully pour the hot chocolate into two mugs.
Sprinkle a little ground cinnamon on top. Mmm, good!

 ## Customs Around the World

Feed the Camels

In countries where Spanish is spoken, on the eve
of *El Dia de Reyes* (Three Kings Day), children put
freshly cut grass in a shoebox under their beds for
the Wise Men's camels to eat. Sometime during
the night, *Los Reyes* arrive and quietly leave gifts
for the children while their camels enjoy their
snack. Does this tradition sound like any other
Christmas traditions that you know about?
Do you leave any food out on Christmas Eve?

Christmas Bird Feeder

❄ ❄ ❄

What you need:

* ❋ Plastic milk bottle with lid, half-gallon (2 L), rinsed and dried
* ❋ Scissors (for grown-up use only)
* ❋ Tempera paint, assorted colors, in separate jar lids
* ❋ Paintbrushes
* ❋ 2 pencils
* ❋ Birdseed
* ❋ String or yarn

step 1

What you do:

1. Ask a grown-up to cut out window openings on all four sides of the plastic milk bottle. Beneath each opening, cut out a hole wide enough for a pencil to fit through.

2. Decorate the milk bottle with paint.

3. Poke the pencils through the holes so they crisscross for a perch. Fill the plastic bottle with birdseed. Secure string or ribbon under the lid and hang from a tree.

QUICK & EASY

Ask a grown-up to help you spread peanut butter over a stale bagel. Put the bagel in a brown lunch bag with about a half-cup (125 ml) of birdseed. Shake the bag until the bagel is coated with seed. Remove the bagel from the bag and then shake off any excess seed. Thread yarn through the bagel and hang it from a tree.

WAITING GAMES

Decorate a Christmas Tree for the Birds: Trim a tree for the birds in your yard or neighborhood by hanging up strings of cranberries, raisins, and popcorn and suet cakes (see For-the-BIRDS CAKE, page 85) from the branches. Put out lint that you collect from the dryer and pieces of unraveled yarn from sweaters to help the birds put some added warmth in their nests. The happy birds will thank you by fluttering around and singing their cheerful songs!

 LITTLE HANDS STORY CORNER™

Animal Habitats by Judy Press
Make Your Own Birdhouses and Feeders by Robyn Haus
Kids' Easy-to-Create Wildlife Habitats by Emily Stetson

All Wrapped Up!

Holiday gifts are waiting,
They're such a beautiful sight —
Tied in bows and ribbons,
Wrapped up nice and tight.

Everybody's wondering,
(But no one can decide),
What wonderful surprises
Are waiting tucked inside!

Snowy-Day Wrapping Paper

❄

What you need:

- ❄ 1 sheet of newspaper
- ❄ 1 sheet of tissue paper, any bright color
- ❄ White tempera paint, in a jar lid or container
- ❄ Cardboard tube, any size (cut longer tubes into about 4-inch [10 cm] segments)
- ❄ Plastic bottle cap (as from milk containers)
- ❄ Fine black marker
- ❄ Old toothbrush

Snowmen are a welcome sign of winter fun, so print some on colorful tissue paper to wrap Christmas gifts and winter treats!

What you do:

1. Spread some newspaper. Lay the tissue paper on it. To make the snowman's round base, dip the end of the cardboard tube into the white paint and press onto the tissue paper, making a circle.

2. To make the snowman's mid-section, dip the rim of the bottle cap into the white paint and press above the larger base circle. Repeat with the same bottle cap, placing a circle above the midsection, to make the snowman's head.

3. Draw on the snowman's arms, face, buttons, and scarf with the marker.

4. Repeat Steps 1, 2, and 3 for as many snowmen as you want.

5. Dip the toothbrush into the white paint, turn it so the bristles are pointing down at the tissue paper, and then draw your finger across the bristles to create snow. What beautiful wrapping paper!

QUICK **&** EASY ▪ ˩ ▪ ˩ ▪ ˩ ▪ ˩ ▪ ˩ ▪ ˩ ▪

Ask a grown-up to help you cut a kitchen sponge into a holiday shape (bell, tree, wreath, or candle). Dip the sponge in tempera paint and press onto construction paper. Use this pretty paper to wrap gifts for your family and friends.

WAITING GAMES

Put on a Family Play: Choose a favorite holiday story to act out with other family members. Give everyone a role to play. Have one person read the story from a book, while each actor acts out his character's part. Put on the play the night before your holiday celebration!

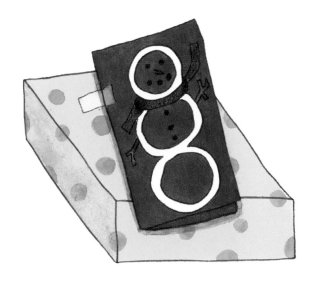

Make Snowmen Gift Tags: Fold 3-inch (7.5 cm) strips of colorful construction-paper scraps in half. Using a bottle cap to make prints, dip the caps first in white tempera paint and then print on the tag (three stacked circles per snowman). Open the tag and ask a grown-up to help you write the words "To" and "From" and the names. Tape to the gift.

Little Hands Kids Say ...™

Samantha and Hannah S. from Philadelphia tell us, "We use the funny pages from our newspaper to wrap presents. It's great because the person who gets the gift can read the comics after they open the package. It's like two gifts in one!"

LITTLE HANDS STORY CORNER™

Giving by Shirley Hughes

Holiday Gift Bag

What you need:

- ❄ Cereal-box cardboard
- ❄ Pencil
- ❄ Child-safety scissors
- ❄ Holiday wrapping paper, recycled
- ❄ White or brown paper lunch bag
- ❄ White glue
- ❄ Ribbon
- ❄ Transparent tape
- ❄ Zipper-style plastic bag

step 2

What you do:

1. To make the templates, draw three or four shapes, such as a tree, a star, and a snowman on the cereal-box cardboard. Cut out the shapes.

2. Trace the shapes onto the back, non-printed side of the holiday wrapping paper, and then cut out the shapes.

3. Glue the wrapping-paper shapes, colorful side up, onto the front and back of the lunch bag.

4. Tape a ribbon to both sides of the bag for a handle. Fill the bag with Christmas surprises such as pencils and erasers, a small pad of paper, some markers, a gift certificate to a favorite bookstore, or a stack of homemade holiday cards (see pages 25–42).

P.S. To save your holiday-shape templates, keep them in a zipper-style plastic bag, and store in a shoe box with other templates to use again.

QUICK & EASY

Use markers and crayons to draw holiday designs on paper lunch bags. Glue on scraps of ribbon and shiny paper for decorations (a combination of tissue-paper scraps and shiny foil-paper scraps is especially festive!).

WAITING GAMES

Christmas Countdown: Put number magnets on a refrigerator door to show the December calendar. Remove a number each day until it's Christmas.

Little Hands Kids Say ...™

Kevin C. from Carlisle, Pennsylvania, says, "My dad puts a little present in a small box. Then he puts the small box inside a bigger box. He puts that box into a bigger box and then into another big box. It's so much fun to open all the boxes and find a little present inside."

Sweet-Smelling Sachets: Tuck cinnamon sticks, cloves, and grapefruit, orange, or lemon peel in a small square of fabric. Gather the corners and secure with a rubber band or ribbon. Place the *sachet*, or scented bag, in a holiday gift bag or in a Christmas stocking. The recipient can then put it in his room or under his pillow for the sweet smell of Christmastime.

An Act of Kindness

Holiday gift bags make nice surprises any time of year. It sure would be nice of you to make a gift bag for a friend or neighbor who is sick. Ask a grown-up to help you fill it (a grown-up might enjoy some tea bags and a few cookies in a bag) and deliver it to the sick person's home.

Christmas-Ball Gift Tag

This gift tag is in the shape of a Christmas ball, but you can shape
and decorate yours like a tree, angel, "Rudolph," or whatever you'd like!

What you need:

* ❄ Newspaper
* ❄ Construction-paper scraps
* ❄ Child-safety scissors
* ❄ Pen or pencil
* ❄ White glue
* ❄ Sparkling confetti
* ❄ Hole punch
* ❄ Ribbon

LITTLE HANDS STORY CORNER™

Tree of Cranes by Allen Say

What you do:

1. Spread out the newspaper. Cut out a 4" (10 cm) square from a scrap of construction paper. Fold the square in half, and using scissors, cut a half-circle shape around the three open sides of the square. Do not cut along the fold line.

2. Open up the half circle. Ask a grown-up to help you write the words "To" and "From," and the names.

3. Decorate the circle like a sparkling Christmas ball by dabbing an area with glue and sprinkling on some sparkling confetti. Repeat as you wish. Let dry. Shake off any excess confetti.

4. Punch a hole at the top of the ornament tag and thread ribbon through the hole to tie on the gift tag.

QUICK & EASY

Cut out gift tags from old holiday greeting cards. Punch a hole in one end and thread a piece of ribbon or yarn through to tie the tag onto a gift.

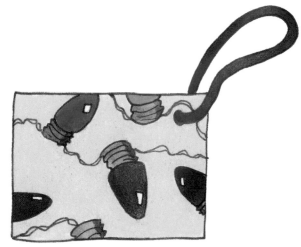

WAITING GAMES

Trace-Your-Hands Gift Tags:
Trace your hands on holiday-colored construction paper. Cut out each hand shape and punch a hole in one side. Write the name of the person the gift is for on each handprint and use ribbon to tie it onto the gift.

Make an Envelope Gift Tag:
Seal a regular business-sized envelope closed, then cut it in half the short way. Punch a hole in the corner of one half. Decorate with holiday designs. Cut out a square from the second half. Ask a grown-up to help you write a greeting on the square and slip the note inside the pocket of the first half. Thread ribbon through the hole to tie on the gift tag.

YUMMY TREATS

Edible Gift-Tag Cookies

Cookie dough, homemade or store-bought
Tube icing for writing

Materials: rolling pin (or substitute); waxed paper; cookie cutters; small wooden spoon; cookie sheet; metal spatula; cooling rack

Yield: 1 batch

Preheat oven as directed on recipe or package. Roll out homemade or store-bought cookie dough to half-inch (5 mm) thick. Use cookie cutters to make a shaped cookie gift tag, or cut out the shape of a rectangular gift tag from the dough. Poke a hole in one corner with the end of the wooden spoon's handle. After the cookies are baked and have cooled, use icing in a tube to write a greeting or a name on the gift-tag cookie.

Three Kings Gift Container

❄ ❄ ❄

What you need:

- ❄ Cardboard oatmeal container or potato-chip canister, with lid
- ❄ Wrapping paper, recycled, solid color
- ❄ Transparent tape
- ❄ Cotton balls or batting
- ❄ White glue
- ❄ Construction-paper scraps, brown, yellow, or white
- ❄ Child-safety scissors
- ❄ Black marker
- ❄ 1 sheet of tissue paper
- ❄ Shiny (foil) wrapping paper, solid color
- ❄ Sequins or beads (optional)
- ❄ Small gifts such as pencils, erasers, crayons, markers, and playing cards

Note to adults: If using small beads or sequins, please evaluate children's readiness to handle without putting in their mouths.

What you do:

1. Cover the container in solid-color wrapping paper. Tape to secure. Glue cotton batting on top of the lid.

2. Cut out the king's face from the construction-paper scraps and glue it onto the top one-third of the container as shown. Cut out the beard from cotton batting and glue it onto the middle third of the container. Draw on the face, hands, and arms.

3. Cut out a tissue-paper robe and tape it onto the back of the container. Cut out a big crown from the shiny wrapping paper and tape it around the complete top of the container. Glue on sequins or beads to decorate the crown if you like.

4. Fill the container with small gifts or homemade treats. Put on lid.

Cover an oatmeal container with gift wrap or construction paper. If a solid color, glue on Christmas pictures from old magazines. If a pattern, glue on small pieces of ribbon or narrow streamers of tissue paper. Add some small surprises and cover with lid, topped with a bow.

WAITING GAMES

Ask a grown-up to read the story of *The Gift of the Magi* by O. Henry. Then do something nice for someone.

Listen to Henry Wadsworth Longfellow's poem "The Three Kings."

With a grown-up's permission, go to http://washingtonmo.com/Christmas/lyric/1058.htm to hear the song "We Three Kings." If you don't know the words, hum the melody.

Giving and Receiving Gifts

Gifts play a part in Christmas as suggested by the Three Wise Men. Gifts also play a part in *Hanukkah*, the Jewish holiday celebrated in late November or December. Different family and cultural traditions determine when the gifts are opened.

The *Twelfth Night* of Christmas, celebrated by Christians on January 6th, is also called *Three Kings' Day* and *Epiphany*. In Italy, Mexico, and other Latin countries, children fill their shoes, beside their beds, with hay to feed the Three Kings' camels. The next morning, they awake to find gifts left for them, it is said, by the Three Kings.

In England, Australia, New Zealand, and Canada, another gift-giving day, called *Boxing Day*, is celebrated on the first weekday after Christmas. This is the time when friends and family exchange gifts, and also give gifts to organizations and people who are in need. A favorite Dutch custom is for each family member to receive the first or last letter of his or her name in chocolate. What a nice way to personalize a gift!

 LITTLE HANDS STORY CORNER™

Hurray for Three Kings' Day!
by Lori Marie Carlson

When does your family open gifts?
Anne and John W. from Charlotte, Vermont, open gifts on Christmas morning. "First my brother and I have a small breakfast snack in our rooms, such as some cereal and a muffin. Then, at the agreed upon time, we wake our parents, put on some Christmas music, make some cocoa, and open a few gifts. We stop to have brunch and to play with our toys. Then, we finish opening gifts and we all help to clean up the paper and make Christmas dinner. In the evening after dinner, we open our stockings! It's always the best day!"

An Act of Kindness

Most people love to see photos of themselves. Look through the photographs that were taken of you and your family and friends throughout the year. Ask permission to use or to make a copy of a photo that has people in it from your neighborhood or at school. Paste the photo on a piece of construction paper and put the year on it. Then, give it as a thoughtful surprise. Someone will be very happy to know that you were thinking of him or her!

Paper-Bag Piñata

❄ ❄ ❄

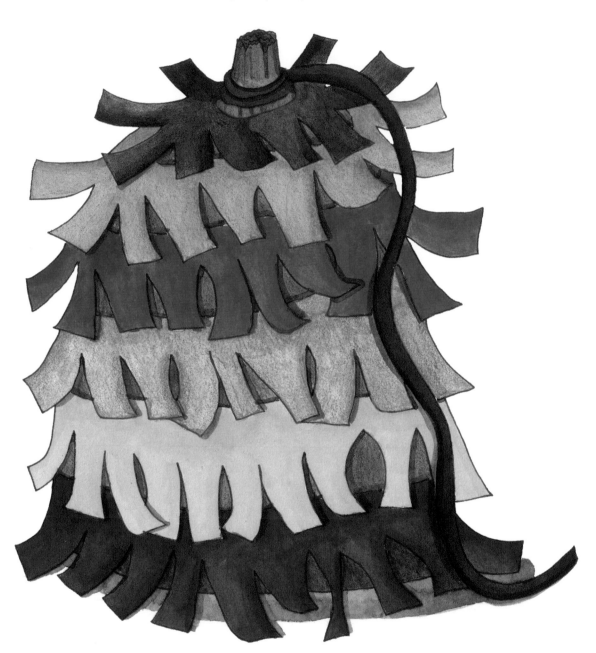

What you need:

- ❄ Brown paper lunch bag
- ❄ Candy and small toys
- ❄ Strips of tissue paper, about
  2" x 4" (5 x 10 cm), assorted colors
- ❄ Child-safety scissors
- ❄ White glue
- ❄ Rubber band
- ❄ Ribbon or string

What you do:

1. Fill the paper bag half-full with candy and small toys. (Make sure all of the candy is in the bag, so that younger children won't pick it up and put it in their mouths).

2. Cut a fringe along the bottom edges of the strips of tissue paper. Starting at the bottom of the bag, glue strips all around the bag, working your way up to the top.

3. Wrap a rubber band around the top of the bag and close tightly. Tie ribbon or string around the top.

4. Now you are ready to play the PIÑATA GAME (see page 80.)

(see page 80.)

QUICK & EASY

Decorate a big glass jar with stickers and some ribbon. Then, fill it with jellybeans or Christmas M&M's. Ask all of your friends to guess how many pieces of candy are in the jar. Write down every guess along with the person's name. On the night before Christmas, wash and dry your hands, and then count the candies. The person who comes closest to the correct number without going over wins the whole candy jar! And in the spirit of Christmas, we know that the winner will share the candy with all!

LITTLE HANDS STORY CORNER™

The Night of Las Posadas by Tomie de Paola

¡Mexico! 40 Activities to Experience Mexico Past & Present by Susan Milord

Customs Around the World

Join the Parade!

In Mexico, children take part in *Las Posadas* (las-poe-SAH-dahs). (See page 105.) Each day from December 16th until Christmas Eve, friends and neighbors gather together for a parade led by two children carrying small figures of Mary and Joseph. At the end of the procession, they are all welcomed into a neighbor's home for a celebration. Sometimes they play the PIÑATA GAME (this page). Wouldn't it be fun to go to a party every night before Christmas?

WAITING GAMES

Make (and Write) Thank-You Notes: Draw a small stamp-sized box with your last name's initial on it. Then, make copies of your drawn initial stamp and cut out. Fold sheets of paper into note cards and paste your initial stamps to the front of the cards. 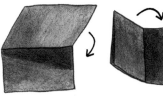 With a grown-up's help, write a sentence or two of thanks for a gift you received, or draw a "thank-you" picture on the inside of the card. Give a card to each person who gave you a gift, or ask a grown-up to mail the cards.

Play the PIÑATA GAME: Ask a grown-up to hang the piñata (peen-YAHT-uh) so it is almost out of reach. Using a cardboard tube or a plastic bat, everyone takes a turn swinging at the piñata, trying to break it open. Once it is broken, everyone gets to pick up some of the toys and candies.

A *buñuelo* (bu-NYWE-lo) is like Mexican fried bread, or a fritter or fried dough. Since the PIÑATA GAME (see page 80) is from Mexico, it would be fun to make a Mexican treat to eat while you make your piñata.

Easy Mexican Buñuelos

1 package of flour tortillas
Oil for frying
Sugar
Cinnamon

Materials: frying pan; spatula; paper towels

Yield: number of tortillas in package

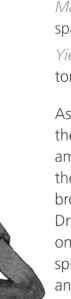

Ask a grown-up to fry the tortillas in a small amount of hot oil until they are crisp and brown on both sides. Drain the fried tortillas on paper towels. Then, sprinkle them with sugar and cinnamon. Once they are slightly cooled, gobble them up!

Let It Snow!

The clouds are starting to gather,
The sky is turning gray.
The weather forecast tells us
That snow is on its way.

Get out your boots and mittens,
Grab the sled that's new.
It's going to be a snow day,
Which means no school for you!

Red Cardinal in Winter

There's nothing quite as beautiful as a pair of red cardinals sitting in a snow-covered evergreen tree. It is such a surprise to see them happily eating at a bird feeder, too.

What you need:

- ❄ Small white paper plate
- ❄ Thin black marker or black pen
- ❄ Brown marker or crayon
- ❄ Cotton balls
- ❄ White glue
- ❄ Red tempera paint, in a small jar lid
- ❄ Small paintbrush

What you do:

1. Draw bare tree branches on the plate with a black marker. Color the branches brown. Glue on bits of cotton for snow.

2. Dip a finger into the red paint and press onto the plate to make two attached circles for the cardinal's body.

3. Draw on the cardinal's beak, tail, wing, and an eye with the black marker. Use the paintbrush to fill in the wing, tail, and beak with red paint. Let dry.

To make a cardinal in snow, open and flatten a coffee filter, then fold it in half, then in half again … and again … and again.

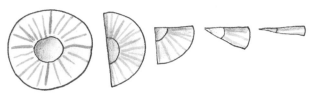

Cut tiny triangles into both sides of the filter. Open the coffee-filter snowflake and glue it onto blue construction paper. Cut a bird shape out of a red construction-paper scrap and glue it onto the snowflake.

WAITING GAMES

Look for a Red Cardinal Outdoors: If you live in the eastern half or northwestern region of North America, you may very well have a pair of cardinals living in your area. The *male*, or boy, cardinal is bright red all over and the *female*, or girl, cardinal is grayish-tan with a red tail and wings. They are usually together, flying low in the woods and visiting feeders. They love to eat black-oil sunflower seeds at feeders. Listen to the cardinal's song: *what-cheer*, *what-cheer*, or *teew, teew*. Its call sounds like *tchip, tchip*.

"We hang our bird feeders every year on Thanksgiving Day. It is up to us to keep them full until early spring. It's an easy job. My sister and I keep a journal of every kind of bird we see. Sometimes it is hard to identify them, but the cardinals are easy to spot. He's bright red and she's a duller gray color, but together they are our favorites!" says Susannah W. of Lewiston, Maine.

YUMMY TREATS

For-the-Birds Cake

2 cups (500 ml) shortening (bacon fat or suet)
1 cup (250 ml) chunky peanut butter
1 cup (250 ml) oatmeal
1 cup (250 ml) birdseed

Materials: large saucepan; dry measuring cups; wooden spoon; muffin tin; paper muffin cups; string

Yield: 12 bird cakes

Ask a grown-up to melt the shortening and peanut butter in the large saucepan. Remove the saucepan from the heat and add the oatmeal and birdseed. Mix well, then pour into the paper-lined muffin tin. Allow to cool overnight. Take the paper off the cakes and attach a string to one or two cakes. Hang outdoors. Save the rest for bird treats on other winter days.

 LITTLE HANDS STORY CORNER™

Bird Tales from Near & Far by Susan Milord
(folk tales plus related activities)

Really Cool Igloo!

What you need:

- ❄ Styrofoam plate
- ❄ Child-safety scissors
- ❄ 1 sheet of blue construction paper
- ❄ White glue
- ❄ Black marker
- ❄ White chalk

What you do:

1. Cut the Styrofoam plate in half. Using one half, cut off its wide edge, leaving the half-circle center. Glue the center onto the middle of the blue construction paper. Then, cut the remaining edge into block shapes to look like ice blocks. Set them aside.

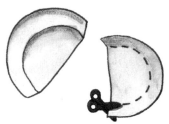

2. Using the remaining half plate, cut out a small rounded opening for a door. Glue the half with the door face-down on top of the plate that is on the blue paper. (It should look as if the door is open.)

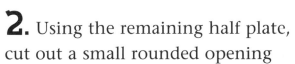

3. Glue the Styrofoam blocks that you saved onto the outside of the igloo. Use the marker and chalk to draw a winter scene around your igloo.

QUICK & EASY

Press a kitchen sponge into white tempera paint. Print blocks of ice onto a large cardboard box for an instant igloo.

WAITING GAMES

Build an Outdoor Igloo: Fill washed and rinsed cardboard milk cartons with water. Leave the cartons outdoors to freeze. When frozen solid, peel away the cardboard. Use the blocks to build a wall. *Hint:* Stick the blocks together with water.

"My mom and I bring in my neighbor's mail and newspaper, and we check on her every day in winter," says Jonathan M. of Reading, Massachusetts. "We shovel her walk and in bad weather, we shop for her groceries and cat food, too."

LITTLE HANDS STORY CORNER™

Mama, Do You Love Me? by Barbara M. Joosse

An Act of Kindness

When the sidewalks get icy, it is time to help your older neighbors. Why? First, it is a nice thing to do, and second, when older people slip on ice, they are more likely to break some bones than younger people. So, be a good neighbor and bring their newspapers to their front doors, too.

Jolly Snowman

❄ ❄

step 1

step 2

What you need:

- ❄ Old sock
- ❄ Child-safety scissors
- ❄ White Styrofoam cup
- ❄ Rubber band
- ❄ White glue
- ❄ Pom-pom
- ❄ Black and orange construction-paper scraps
- ❄ Hole punch (optional)
- ❄ Ribbon
- ❄ Thin, short twigs

What you do:

1. Cut away the bottom half of the sock, reserving just the sock's cuff to use. Turn the cup upside down and stretch the cuff partially over the cup, about one-fourth of the way. Secure the remaining cuff that is sticking up with the rubber band. Glue on the pom-pom.

2. Cut out or hole punch tiny circles from the black construction paper.

Glue them onto the snowman for eyes, mouth, and buttons. Repeat with the orange construction paper for an orange nose. Glue the ribbon around the center of the cup.

3. Ask a grown-up to help you poke the twigs into the sides of the cup for arms.

Cover a tabletop with newspaper and lay a piece of waxed paper over that. Use a can of non-aerosol foam shaving cream to make a tabletop snowman.

WAITING GAMES

Discover Snowflakes: Catch snowflakes on a dark-colored piece of construction paper or a dark-colored mitten. Look at them through a magnifying glass to see their unique designs. Remember, no two snowflakes are exactly alike! Can you imagine that?

Marshmallow Snowman

3 large marshmallows
Mini chocolate chips, candy corn,
shoestring licorice
Cake icing

Materials: plastic straw

Yield: 1 marshmallow snowman

Push marshmallows onto the straw. Stick on the candy using the cake icing as glue. Use the chocolate chips for the snowman's eyes, mouth, and buttons. Use the candy corn for a nose and the licorice for a scarf.

 Little Hands Kids Say ...™

"My sisters, cousins, and I build a huge snowman every winter when we have a snow day from school. Afterwards, we come in the house freezing cold and soaking wet, leaving our snowy clothes by the woodstove. My mom always gives us hot cocoa and cookies, as we settle in to watch *Frosty the Snowman*. And every time, we sing along to the final chorus of 'Frosty the Snowman' with Burl Ives," says Michael P. from Pittsburgh, Pennsylvania.

 LITTLE HANDS STORY CORNER™

The Snowman by Raymond Briggs
Snowflake Bentley by Jacqueline Briggs Martin

Wintertime Skier

❄ ❄ ❄

What you need:

- ❄ Toilet-paper tube
- ❄ 2 strips of construction paper, 1½" x 6" (3.5 x 15 cm), 2 colors
- ❄ Transparent tape
- ❄ Child-safety scissors
- ❄ Construction-paper scrap: brown, yellow, or white
- ❄ White glue
- ❄ Marker
- ❄ Tissue paper, 4" x 6" (10 x 15 cm)
- ❄ 2 Popsicle sticks
- ❄ Foil-paper scraps
- ❄ 2 toothpicks
- ❄ Sharp pointed tool (for grown-up use only)

What you do:

1. Wrap half the toilet-paper tube in one strip of construction paper, then wrap the other half in the second strip. Tape to hold.

2. Cut out the skier's head from the construction-paper scrap. Glue it onto the tube, as shown. Draw on the face, arms, and hands.

3. Make a single fold in the long end of the tissue paper and glue the folded end around the top of the tube. Twist the end of the tissue together for a hat.

4. Tape the two Popsicle sticks side-by-side. Tape the skier onto the sticks.

5. Cut out two small circles from the foil paper. Poke a toothpick through each circle to make poles. Ask a grown-up to poke two holes in each of the skier's hands. Insert one toothpick through the holes in one hand and repeat with the other toothpick and hand.

QUICK & EASY

Cut out a pair of **"skis"** from cardboard. Attach the skis to your feet with a heavy-duty rubber band. Now, hold onto long, cardboard gift-wrap tubes (for ski poles) and practice your ski moves on a flat, soft surface.

WAITING GAMES

Paint the Snow! On a snowy day, add a few drops of food coloring to a pail of water. Then go outdoors and dip a wide paintbrush into the water. Now, "paint" designs, shapes, and scenes in the snow.

Mitten Note Cards

This craft is fun to do and very useful too! It can be given as a gift, or used as a tree ornament, place cards at a dinner table, or for note cards, as shown here.

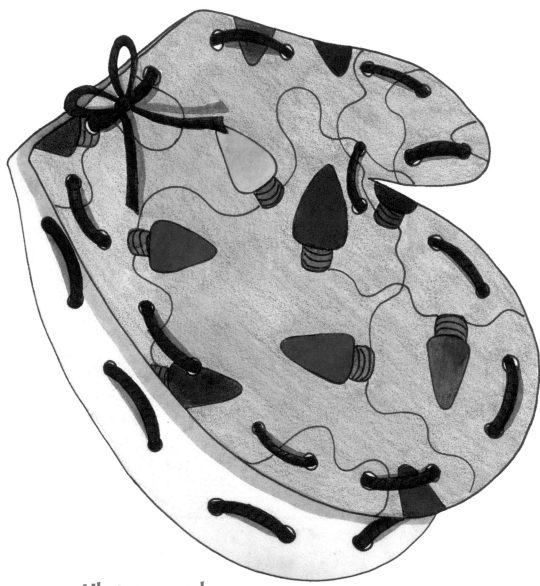

What you need:

- ❄ 2 recycled cards
- ❄ Child-safety scissors
- ❄ Pencil
- ❄ Hole punch
- ❄ Yarn
- ❄ Different-colored yarn than above or thin ribbon

What you do:

1. Cut away the backs of the two cards, reserving just the cards' fronts for this craft. Turn one card's front over (picture-side down) and draw the shape of a mitten on it. Cut out.

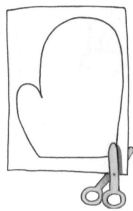

2. Flip the mitten over to picture-side up and trace it onto the non-picture-side of the second card's front. Cut out.

3. Punch holes around three edges of both mittens, but not along the top of the cuff. Doing one mitten at a time, thread yarn through the holes.

4. Punch two holes along both mittens' cuffs. Now, thread a ribbon or different-colored piece of yarn through the cuff holes and tie the mittens together.

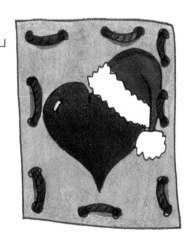

QUICK & EASY

Cut away the back of a holiday card. Punch holes around the front of the card and sew with yarn. Ask a grown-up to help you write a note.

Ice-Cream Snowball

Vanilla ice cream
Shredded sweetened coconut or
multicolored sprinkles

Materials: plastic wrap; ice cream scoop

Yield: 1 snowball

Wrap a scoop of softened ice cream in plastic wrap. Shape the ice cream into a ball and put it into the freezer to harden. When ready to serve, unwrap the ice-cream ball and roll it in the shredded coconut or sprinkles for an indoor snowball treat.

WAITING GAMES

Mitten Match: Pile several pairs of different-sized and different-textured mittens and gloves in a large box or a bag. Players close their eyes and take turns reaching into the box. Using their sense of touch only, players try to pull out a matching pair of mittens. If the mittens match, then the player puts the pair aside. If they don't match, the player puts them back into the box. Now the next person takes a turn.

LITTLE HANDS STORY CORNER™

The Mitten Tree by Candace Christiansen
Missing Mittens by Stuart J. Murphy

An Act of Kindness

Warm Hands Make Warm Hearts!

Ask a grown-up to help you string a clothesline across a big room in school, on your front lawn in your neighborhood, or at your place of worship. Leave some clothespins on the line and hang one pair of new or used mittens (that you no longer need). Put up a sign, as shown below.

Now, watch how others begin adding to the clothesline. When one line is full, add another, then another. On the last day of collecting, take a picture of all of the mittens and send it to your local newspaper. Then, box up the mittens and ask a grown-up to help you bring them to a shelter, the Salvation Army, a Goodwill center, or other nearby clothing distribution center. Great job! You've done a thoughtful act of kindness!

December Pop-Up Diorama

What you need:

- ❄ Shoe box with lid
- ❄ Holiday wrapping paper, recycled, or brown paper bag, cut open so flat, decorated with markers
- ❄ Transparent tape
- ❄ White glue
- ❄ Cotton balls or batting
- ❄ Holiday cards, recycled, about 8
- ❄ Child-safety scissors
- ❄ Utility knife (for grown-up use only)
- ❄ Popsicle or craft sticks

What you do:

1. Wrap the shoe box in the wrapping paper or brown paper, and tape to hold. Glue cotton across the top of the shoe box.

2. To make the wintry scene background, choose cards that have winter scenes on them, if possible. Cut off the backs of the used holiday cards. Tape some of the card fronts across the back edge of the shoe box for a background.

3. To make pop-up objects and people for your diorama, choose card fronts with pictures of people, dogs, trees, and other festive objects. Cut out the shapes and tape each one onto a Popsicle stick.

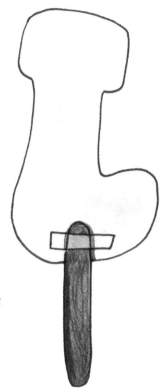

4. Ask a grown-up to poke slits in the top of the box where you would like to place your pop-ups. Insert a Popsicle stick with pop-up into each slit.

LITTLE HANDS STORY CORNER™

When Winter Comes
by Nancy Van Laan & Susan Gaber

The Biggest Snowball Ever! by John Rogan

QUICK & EASY

Draw a picture of a December outdoor scene or a traditional indoor Christmas scene with stockings hanging from a fireplace mantle. Then, look through an old magazine for pictures of people, pets, Christmas trees, Santa, or whatever you would like in your picture. Cut them out and paste onto your background drawing.

WAITING GAMES

Create a Holiday Weather Calendar: On each day leading up to the holiday, draw the weather conditions on a calendar. Use symbols such as a cloud, raindrops, snowflakes, or the sun. What will you use to show that it is colder than usual?

Holiday Word Scramble: Write a list of wintry or holiday words, then scramble the letters. Challenge a friend to unscramble the letters and find the words. Here are a few words to get you started (see the answers at the bottom of the page):

1. TIEWNR
2. TASNA
3. WOSN
4. FEL
5. RFI ETER (two words)

1. Winter 2. Santa 3. Snow 4. Elf 5. Fir tree

Santa's Sleigh

❄ ❄ ❄

What you need:

- ❄ Holiday wrapping paper, recycled
- ❄ Cereal box, empty
- ❄ White glue
- ❄ Child-safety scissors
- ❄ 4 Popsicle sticks
- ❄ Aluminum foil or foil gift wrap, recycled
- ❄ Transparent tape
- ❄ Ribbon
- ❄ Boughs, pine cones, candy, and decorations

What you do:

1. Glue wrapping paper onto the front, back, and sides of the cereal box. Ask a grown-up to help cut out the shape of a sleigh.

2. Wrap each Popsicle stick in the foil, and tape them to the bottom of the sleigh for runners.

3. Glue ribbon around the sleigh for decoration. Now, fill your sleigh with evergreen boughs, pinecones, and other decorations.

P.S. You can wrap small jewelry boxes to place in the sleigh to make it look as if there are gifts piled inside.

 LITTLE HANDS STORY CORNER™

The Wild Christmas Reindeer by Jan Brett

QUICK & EASY

Draw a sleigh for Santa on a piece of construction paper. Then cut out pictures of packages, Santa, elves, reindeer, and happy girls and boys to paste around the sleigh. Ask a grown-up to help you write "Ho-Ho-Ho!" across the bottom of your picture.

WAITING GAMES

A Winter Walk: Ask a grown-up to take you outdoors on a winter night when there is fresh snow on the ground. Bring along flashlights and look in the snow for animal tracks. How many different kinds of animal tracks do you see? Are some big and some small? Now look at your footprints in the snow. Are they the biggest ones you see?

Customs Around the World

It's a Lion, a Tiger, a ... Santa?

Do you imagine Santa arriving by sleigh, stopping on rooftops, and buzzing down chimneys? Well, that may be how he is said to arrive in your part of the world, but children around the globe look forward to Santa's arrival in many different ways. In Holland and also in Hawaii, he arrives by boat, and in the African Republic of Ghana, Father Christmas is said to come out of the jungle. In Australia, Santa sometimes is said to arrive on water skis! Sounds as if Santa must be very practical, choosing the means of transportation that works best so he can get gifts to all children everywhere!

Light Up the Night!

Holiday candles flicker,
Menorahs shine so bright;
Kinaras cast a warm glow
On this clear winter's night.

The Christmas star's in the sky,
Luminarias light the way;
Flames flutter in Diwali lamps —
Each holiday's a special day!

Lovely Luminary

❄ ❄ ❄

The custom of lighting *luminarias* (LOO-min-AH-ree-ahs), which are little lanterns placed along a path, came to most of us by way of Mexican Christmas celebrations. They brighten the way for the *Las Posadas* (lahs poh-SAH-thahs) procession. This is when children walk through their neighborhoods reenacting the journey of Mary and Joseph's search for an inn. During Las Posadas, people place luminarias along their streets and the paths leading up to their homes. It looks magical! Now, many Americans use luminarias to light paths to their homes when they are having a party any time of year! Thank you Mexico for sharing your Las Posadas tradition!

What you need:

- ❋ Brown paper bag, lunch size
- ❋ Markers, assorted colors
- ❋ Child-safety scissors
- ❋ Tissue paper
- ❋ Transparent tape
- ❋ 1 cup of sand
- ❋ 1 votive candle
- ❋ Matches (for grown-up use only)

What you do:

1. Keeping the bag folded flat, draw a holiday shape in the center of the paper bag. Then ask a grown-up to help you cut out the shape through both sides of the bag. Decorate the rest of the bag with markers, if you wish.

2. Tape colored tissue paper inside the bag, covering the cutout shapes.

3. Fold down the rim of the bag opening. Add one cup of sand. Push the votive candle into the sand. Ask a grown-up to light the candle.

Note to adults: It is best to use a long lighter to reach inside the bag. Do not, under any circumstances, let a child try to light the votive, and be sure to keep the matches or lighter with you at all times.

Little Hands Kids Say ...™

"On Christmas Eve the people in my neighborhood put luminarias along the street and on the paths going up to their houses. I like the way the whole street is filled with light," says Kristen P. from Santa Fe, New Mexico.

LITTLE HANDS STORY CORNER™

The Legend of the Poinsettia by Tomie dePaola
The Farolitos of Christmas by Rudolfo Anaya

An Act of Kindness

Decorate a grocery-sized bag with holiday or celebration shapes.
Each day before Christmas or any celebration (such as your birthday), place an unopened can or box of food in the bag. The day before the holiday or event, ask a grown-up to help you deliver the food to your local food bank or food shelf.

St. Lucia Candle Wreath

❄ ❄

Swedish people celebrate *Luciadagen* (Loo-SEE-ah-dah-gen), or St. Lucia (Loo-SEE-ah) Day, on December 13th. On this day, the oldest daughter in each household dresses up as St. Lucia, wearing a white gown with a red sash and a crown of candles on her head. She serves her parents a breakfast in bed of special St. Lucia Day buns, called *lussekatter*, and coffee. Boys join in wearing cone-shaped hats decorated with stars. St. Lucia is known as the Queen of Lights, so everyone sings special carols to thank her for bringing them hope during this very dark time of year. It is a special day for all.

What you need:

- ❉ Styrofoam plate
- ❉ Child-safety scissors
- ❉ Strips of green tissue paper, 2" (5 cm) wide
- ❉ Transparent tape
- ❉ Orange or red construction-paper scraps
- ❉ Utility knife (for grown-up use only)

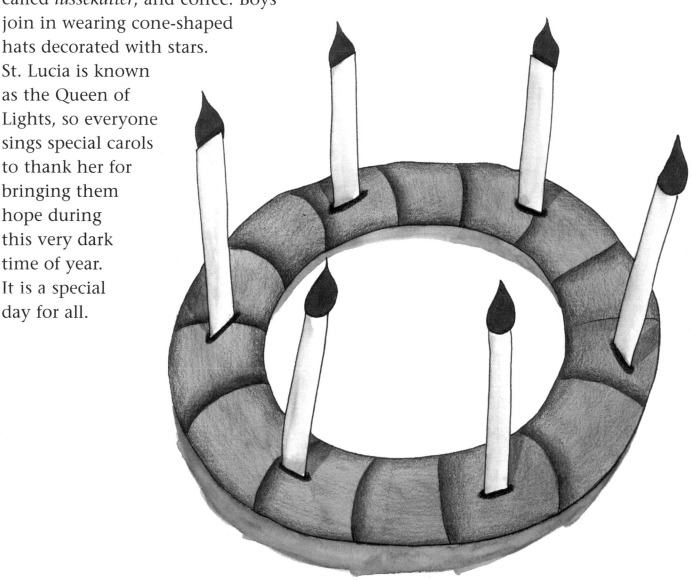

What you do:

1. Ask a grown-up to help you cut out the center of the Styrofoam plate to make a wreath. Wrap the tissue paper strips around the wreath. Tape to hold.

2. Cut out six candles from the leftover plate center. Cut out flames from the construction paper and tape them onto the candles.

3. Ask a grown-up to cut six slits around the wreath for the paper candles. Insert the candles into the slits. Now stand straight, walk tall, and carry the wreath on your head in the tradition of St. Lucia Day.

Little Hands Kids Say ...™

"**Two nights before St. Lucia Day,** we make the dough for *luciapepparkator* (gingerbread) cookies. We put in the spices and the other ingredients, and we refrigerate the dough. Then, on the next night, we roll out the dough and use cookie cutters. Then my dad helps us bake them. They're my favorite cookies," says Scott M. from Hershey, Pennsylvania.

 LITTLE HANDS STORY CORNER™

Children of Noisy Village by Astrid Lindgren

St. Lucia Day Gingerbread Cookies

The Swedish *luciapepparkator* cookies are very special when made from scratch, but you can sample the spices' flavors with this shortcut. The cookies are a delicious reminder that Christmas is coming soon!

1 package store-bought sugar-cookie dough
1/3 cup (75 ml) sugar
1/2 tsp. (2 ml) cinnamon
1/4 tsp. (1 ml) powdered ginger
1/4 tsp. (1 ml) powdered nutmeg

Materials: knife (for grown-up use only); dry measuring cups; measuring spoons; wooden spoon; large plate; baking sheet

Yield: about 30 cookies

Preheat oven according to package directions. Ask a grown-up to slice the cookie dough into cookies. Mix the sugar and spices together on the plate. Press the top of each cookie into the sugar and spice mixture and place on the baking sheet. Bake the cookies according to the package directions.

Mmm! Don't they smell good?

WAITING GAMES

Start a holiday stamp collection with the stamps that arrive on holiday greeting cards. Soak the stamps in warm water to release them, or if they are "sticker" stamps, cut them out. Then arrange your stamp collection in an album and compare the different holiday designs and the places the stamps came from.

Kwanzaa Kinara

Kwanzaa (KWAHN-zah) is a celebration of the African-American culture, community, and family that begins on December 26th. The *kinara* (kee-NAR-ah) is a wooden candleholder used in the weeklong celebration. It holds seven candles, one for each day of Kwanzaa. The black candle stands for the dark-colored skin of the black people of Africa and of African-Americans. The three red candles are to remember the past and present struggles of African-Americans. Three green candles represent hope for the future. The black candle is lit on the first night of Kwanzaa. On the following nights, another candle is added, first a red candle, then a green candle, then a red candle, and so on.

What you need:

- ❋ Styrofoam egg carton, bottom half
- ❋ Child-safety scissors
- ❋ Aluminum foil, recycled
- ❋ 7 plastic straws
- ❋ Black, green, and red tissue paper
- ❋ Glue stick or transparent tape
- ❋ Sparkly pipe cleaners
- ❋ Pencil

What you do:

1. Ask a grown-up to help you cut the egg carton in half the long way. Wrap one half in the aluminum foil.

2. Cut two straws so they are 3" (7.5 cm) long. Cut two straws so they are 4" (10 cm) long. Cut two straws so they are 6" (15 cm) long. Don't cut the last straw.

3. Wrap the tallest straw in black tissue paper. Glue or tape to secure. Wrap one straw of each size in red tissue paper. Glue or tape to secure. Wrap one straw of each size in green tissue paper. Glue or tape to secure.

4. Cut the pipe cleaners into pieces 3" (7.5 cm) long. Bend the pieces into flame shapes (arcs) and insert them into the straws.

5. Ask a grown-up to use a pencil to poke a hole in each section of the egg carton and insert the red and green straws in the order shown in the illustration (see page 110). Insert the black straw in the middle hole.

QUICK & EASY

Cut the bottom of an egg carton in half the long way and wrap it in aluminum foil. Ask a grown-up to poke a hole in the center of each section of the egg carton and then insert red and green crayons for candles. Insert a black crayon in between the middle sections.

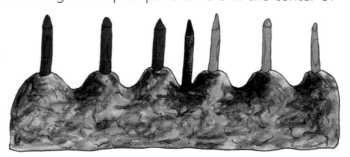

Customs Around the World

Kwanzaa Traditions

The word *Kwanzaa* comes from the African language of *Swahili* (Swa-HEE-lee) and means "first fruit of the harvest." To prepare for the holiday, families place a *mkeka* (mm-KAT-kah), which is a straw mat (see WAITING GAMES below), on the table. A bowl of corn, other vegetables, fruit, and nuts is placed on the mkeka to acknowledge the earth's harvest.

There is a special cup, called a *unity cup*, on the mkeka that each member of the family drinks from, symbolizing the closeness of the family. Then, they share memories and stories from days past.

WAITING GAMES

Make a *Mkeka*, or Kwanzaa Mat: Cut red and green construction paper into strips. Fold a sheet of black construction paper in half. Cut slits across the paper, stopping about 1" (2.5 cm) from the edge. Weave the red and green paper strips in and out of the slits in the black paper and tape the ends to hold. Use your mkeka to decorate your kitchen table in the Kwanzaa tradition (see CUSTOMS AROUND THE WORLD above).

YUMMY TREATS

Harvest Bean Salad for Kwanzaa

1 can, 15-oz. (432 g) corn kernels, drained

1 can, 15-oz. (432 g) black beans, rinsed and drained

1 can, 15-oz. (432 g) cut green beans, drained

1/2 cup (125 ml) each diced red and green peppers

Dressing:
1/4 cup (50 ml) salad oil
1/4 cup (50 ml) sugar
1/2 (125 ml) cup white vinegar
3/4 tsp. (4 ml) ground cumin
11/2 tsp. (7 ml) chili powder
1/2 tsp. (2 ml) salt
1/2 tsp. (2 ml) pepper

Materials: can opener and knife (for grown-up use only); cutting board; large and small mixing bowls; liquid and dry measuring cups; measuring spoons; wire whisk; wooden spoon

Yield: 8 servings

Ask a grown-up to open the cans of vegetables and to help you cut up the red and green peppers. Place the peppers in the large bowl. Add the drained corn, black beans, and green beans. In the small bowl, whisk together all of the salad dressing ingredients. Pour the dressing over the beans and mix with the wooden spoon. Chill the salad in the refrigerator before serving.

Little Hands Kids Say ...™

"Day number six of Kwanzaa is about being creative. I make a Kwanzaa mat from red, green and black construction paper. We put the mat on the kitchen table," Keisha P. from Miami, Ohio, tells us.

In the African language of Swahili, creativity is *kuumba* (koo-OO-mbah). Do you have kuumba?

LITTLE HANDS STORY CORNER™

The Gifts of Kwanzaa by Synthia Saint James

K Is for Kwanzaa: A Kwanzaa Alphabet by Juwanda G. Ford

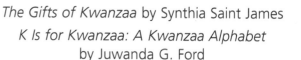

Floating Diwali Candle

Diwali (Di-WA-li, sometimes also Di-VA-li) is the Hindu festival of lights. *Diyas* are lamps made from small clay bowls filled with oil and wicks. They're placed along buildings, pathways, streets, and riverbanks. Some are set afloat in rivers. If the lamps cross safely to the other side, it is seen as a sign of good fortune.

What you need:

- ❋ Toilet-paper tube
- ❋ Child-safety scissors
- ❋ Aluminum foil, recycled
- ❋ Orange or red construction-paper scraps
- ❋ White glue, in small lid or container
- ❋ Paper bowl
- ❋ Markers

What you do:

1. Ask a grown-up to help you cut the toilet-paper tube in half horizontally (across). Wrap one half in the aluminum foil.

2. Cut out a flame from the construction paper and glue it to the inside of the toilet-paper tube for a candle.

3. To decorate the paper bowl, color the top edge of the outside. Dip the bottom of the candle in the glue, and then place it in the center of the bowl. Float the bowl and candle in a pan of shallow water.

 Customs Around the World

During Diwali, wish your **Hindu** friends and neighbors, *"Shubh Deepavali!"* (Shoob di-pa-waa'li), which means "a very happy Diwali."

 Little Hands Kids Say ...™

"On Diwali I go to the temple to celebrate," Vishnu S. from Pittsburgh, Pennsylvania, tells us. "At the altar, I offer different sweets and fruits. One sweet is called *pera*, which is very fruity. I also take bananas, apples, grapes, and many other fruits. I dress in Indian clothes. When I go to the temple, I sing and play the *harmonium*, which is an Indian instrument. We light little lamps called *diyas*, and put at least three in each room."

  **LITTLE HANDS STORY CORNER**™

Lighting a Lamp: A Diwali Story
by Jonny Zucker

Hanukkah Menorah

The Jewish holiday of *Hanukkah* (Ha-NU-kah) is celebrated for eight days. During this time, candles are burned in a special candleholder, called a *menorah* (meh-NOR-ah). Each menorah has nine individual places for candles, with one for the server or leader candle, called the *shammes* (SHAE-mes), and eight more for the eight nights of the holiday. The shammes is lit first and then it's used to light the other candles.

What you need:

- Cereal-box cardboard, 8¹/₂" x 11" (21 x 27.5 cm)
- 1 sheet of construction paper, any color
- White glue
- Utility knife (for grown-up use only)
- 9 Popsicle sticks
- Markers, assorted colors
- Orange or red construction-paper scraps
- Child-safety scissors
- Holiday wrapping paper

What you do:

1. Glue the sheet of construction paper onto the cardboard. Ask a grown-up to cut a row of four slits, 2" (5 cm) from the bottom of the cardboard. Leave a space and cut four more slits. Then cut one slit higher than the others in the middle of the cardboard.

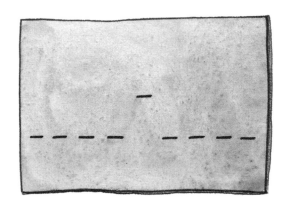

2. Color the Popsicle sticks. Cut out nine red or orange paper flames, and glue them onto one end of each stick. Insert the sticks into the slits.

3. Cut out the shape of a menorah from the wrapping paper. Glue the wrapping-paper menorah shape onto the cardboard.

4. On the first day of Hanukkah, put the shammes candle in the upper slit and insert a Popsicle-stick candle on the left side of the menorah. On each of the eight nights, add a new candle, always adding from the left and working your way across. Tape each candle to the back of the cardboard to hold it in place.

QUICK & EASY

Draw a picture of a menorah on construction paper. Glue on Popsicle sticks for candles, and draw and color in the flames.

WAITING GAMES

How Many Candles in All? On the eight nights of Hanukkah, Jewish people light the candles and let them burn completely out. So, each night they have a new shammes and also all new candles. That means that on Day Three, for example, they light a new shammes plus three new candles. In eight nights, how many candles will they have burned?

Hint: Draw a picture of the menorah with candles on each night. Then count up the candles and you'll have the answer. Ask an older friend to help you because it is a big number! Here, I'll help you get started.

1st night = 2 candles

2nd night = 3 candles

3rd night = 4 candles

Sing along to "I Have a Little Dreidel": With a grown-up's permission, go to http://www.night.net/kids/hanukkah-s-dreidel.html to learn the words.

Customs Around the World

The Hanukkah Story

The Hanukkah story is one of light and of hope. In ancient times, a Jewish temple (where Jewish people go to pray) was attacked and almost all of the oil was spilled or stolen. There was only enough oil left for one night to keep the sacred eternal lamp burning in the temple (it is never supposed to go out). It would take at least eight days to get more oil.

While a group set out to get more oil, miraculously, the oil in the lamp kept burning and burning. It burned for eight days and eight nights, until the people returned with more oil.

In honor of that event, Jewish people around the world celebrate the eight days of Hanukkah by lighting candles in a menorah for eight nights in a row. It is a joyful celebration when songs are sung, gifts are exchanged, and children play games with a *dreidel* (DRAY-dull), a small spinning top.

Hanukkah Applesauce

4 cups (1 L) apples (peeled and sliced)
1 cup (250 ml) water
1/2 cup (125 ml) sugar, or to taste
1 teaspoon lemon juice
Cinnamon (optional)

Materials: saucepan; liquid and dry measuring cups; measuring spoons; wooden spoon; potato masher

Yield: 3 cups of applesauce

Ask a grown-up to help you put all of the ingredients in the saucepan. Cook for about 20 minutes, until the apples are tender, stirring with the wooden spoon. Remove from heat. Mash the cooked apples until they are the consistency you like, either lumpy or smooth. Let the applesauce cool and serve warm, or store in the refrigerator in an airtight container.

P.S. Hanukkah applesauce is especially good with potato pancakes, called *latkes* (LOT- keez)!

An Act of Kindness

Make your mom, dad, or grandparents eight Hanukkah surprises — one for each night! Children often receive one small gift on each night of Hanukkah, but grown-ups often don't receive gifts. They love giving gifts, but don't you think they might enjoy receiving some? You can make some small gifts (see pages 44–63) and you can give them "I-Love-You Cards," too. Cut out a small piece of paper. Ask a grown-up to help you write what gift you are going to give on your card. It can be something like, "Good for setting the table"; "Good for sweeping the porch"; or "Good for playing with the dog." Happy Hanukkah, Everyone!

 LITTLE HANDS STORY CORNER™

Latkes and Applesauce: A Hanukkah Story by Fran Manushkin
Hershel and the Hanukkah Goblins by Eric A. Kimmel

Christmas Star

❄ ❄

The Christmas Star, or the Star of Bethlehem as it is often called, is an important part of the Christmas story. This is the star that shone so brightly over the town of Bethlehem where Mary lay in a manger and Jesus was born.

The Three Wise Men (see activity, pages 74–76) followed this special star and came upon the manger. They brought gifts of gold, frankincense, and myrrh to honor this great event in the history of Christianity.

What you need:

* 2 small white paper plates
* Child-safety scissors
* Markers, assorted colors
* Aluminum foil, recycled
* White glue
* Plastic wrap, in a holiday color
* Transparent tape
* Hole punch
* Ribbon

What you do:

1. Ask a grown-up to help you cut out a star from the center of one plate. Decorate the back of the plate with markers.

2. Place the second plate on the aluminum foil and trace around it. Cut out the foil circle and glue it onto the front of the plate.

3. Tape a piece of plastic wrap across the aluminum foil. Tape the plate with the cutout star upside-down over the foil-covered plate. Punch a hole in the top of the plates. Thread a ribbon through the hole to hang the star.

 ## Customs Around the World

"First Star I See Tonight …"

In Poland, Christmas Eve dinner is served after the first star appears in the sky, symbolizing the Christmas Star and the birth of Christ. Families spend the day cleaning the house and decorating their Christmas tree, then as soon as someone spots the first star, dinner is served. After dinner, gifts are exchanged — there's even something for the family pet! Do you know the story of the holidays you celebrate? If not, ask a grown-up to help you find books about your favorite holidays at the library.

YUMMY TREATS

Peanut-Butter-and-Jelly Star

2 slices of bread
Peanut butter
Jelly, any flavor

Materials: dull knife for spreading; knife for cutting (for grown-up use only); star-shaped cookie cutter (large)

Yield: 1 star-shaped sandwich

Ask a grown-up to help you spread peanut butter and jelly on one slice of bread. Put the second slice of bread on top for a sandwich. Ask a grown-up to help cut away the crusts. Cut out a star from the sandwich using the cookie cutter.

Note to adults: Please use caution when serving anything with peanuts to children other than your own, as some children have severe allergies to peanuts.

Little Hands Kids Say ...™

Do you make a wish upon a star when you see the first star of the night? Matthew, Courtney, and Camryn S. from Brookfield, Connecticut, do. Whoever sees the star first recites this rhyme:

> *Star light,*
> *Star bright,*
> *First star I see tonight.*
> *I wish I may,*
> *I wish I might,*
> *Have this wish,*
> *I wish tonight.*

Courtney says, "Then, I make a special wish." What would your wish be?

 LITTLE HANDS STORY CORNER™

The Christmas Star by Marcus Pfister
Draw Me a Star by Eric Carle

Chinese New Year Dragon

❄ ❄

Every year, the Chinese New Year holiday ends with a dragon
parade. A dancing dragon made of paper, silk, and bamboo is carried
through the streets, followed by people playing drums and gongs.
Fireworks are set off to send out the old year and welcome in the new.
On New Year's Eve, families gather to celebrate and eat a big meal.
Then all the children are given small red envelopes called
lai-see (lee-see), with good-luck money tucked inside.

What you need:

❄ Brown grocery-sized bag

❄ Child-safety scissors

❄ Markers, assorted colors

❄ Tissue paper, any color

❄ Glue stick

What you do:

1. Ask a grown-up to help you cut away the top three-fourths of the paper bag and, with the bag upside down, to cut out openings for eyes.

2. Draw a dragon's face on the bag.

3. Cut the tissue paper into strips and cut out fringe. Glue the strips onto the bag (the more strips you have, the more fun your dragon mask will be).

Little Hands Kids Say ...™

"**On the Chinese New Year's Eve, we have a big family meal.** Then all of the children receive small red envelopes called *lai-see*. Inside is good-luck money. On New Year's Day, we always visit our grandparents. This is a real family holiday," says Jeff C. from Brooklyn, New York.

Customs Around the World

The Chinese Lunar Calendar!

The exact date each year for the Chinese New Year is determined by the Chinese lunar calendar, which is based on the cycles of the moon. It is celebrated on the first day of the first moon of the lunar calendar, which usually falls in early February. Thus, the Chinese New Year is associated with bringing light into the night, too.

Chinese tradition says that there is a 12-year repeating cycle during which a different animal represents each year. Some Chinese people believe that you will have the characteristics of the animal sign of your birth year. Here are some of the things, for example, a search of Google said about people who are born in the Year of the Tiger: Tiger people are "courageous and powerful," and "daring fighters." They are also "sensitive, given to deep thinking, and capable of great sympathy."

Is that how you would describe a tiger's personality — if it were a person? What characteristics do you think you share with the animals below?

Year of the Rat

Year of the Ox

Year of the Tiger

Year of the Rabbit

Year of the Dragon

Year of the Snake

Year of the Horse

Year of the Goat

Year of the Monkey

Year of the Rooster

Year of the Dog

Year of the Pig

Crafts by Skill Level

The increase in degree of difficulty indicates that slightly more advanced fine motor skill capabilities are needed, as well as an ability to remain on task for slightly longer time periods. Children doing these craft projects will need varying amounts of adult help, depending on each child's skill level. All children will need adult supervision.

Easy ❄

Medium ❄ ❄

Challenging ❄ ❄ ❄

Index

More Good Books from Williamson

Welcome to Williamson Books! Our books are available from your bookseller or directly from Williamson Books at Ideals Publications. Please see below for ordering information or to visit our website. Thank you.

All books are suitable for children ages 3 through 7, and are 120 to 128 pages, 10 x 8 or 8.5 x 11, $12.95, unless otherwise noted.

★ ✦ ★ More *Little Hands*® Books by Judy Press! ✦ ★ ✦

Parent's Guide Classic Award
Real Life Award
The Little Hands ART BOOK
Exploring Arts & Crafts with
2- to 6-Year-Olds

Parents' Choice Recommended
Teachers' Choice Family Award
Sea Life Art & Activities
Creative Experiences for
3- to 7-Year-Olds

*Learning Magazine Teachers' Choice*SM
Award for the Family
Animal Habitats
Learning about North American
animals & plants thru art, science
& creative play

ForeWord Magazine Children's Book
of the Year Finalist
All Around Town
Exploring Your Community
Through Craft Fun

American Institute of Physics
Science Writing Award
Early Childhood News Directors'
Choice Award
Science Play!
Beginning Discoveries for
2- to 6-Year-Olds
by Jill Frankel Hauser

Parents' Choice Gold Award
Fun with My Five Senses
by Sarah Williamson

Parents' Choice Approved
Paper Plate Crafts
by Laura Check

Parents' Choice Recommended
At the Zoo!
Explore the Animal World with
Craft Fun

Parents' Choice Approved
The Little Hands
Big Fun Craft Book
Creative Fun for 2- to 6-Year-Olds

Around-The-World
Art & Activities
Visiting the 7 Continents through
Craft Fun

Art Starts for Little Hands!
Fun Discoveries for 3- to
7-Year-Olds

Parent's Guide Children's Media Award
Alphabet Art
With A to Z Animal Art &
Fingerplays

Parents' Choice Approved Award
Little Hands Create!
by Mary D. Dall

Little Hands®
Celebrate America!
Learning about the U.S.A.
Through Crafts & Activities
by Jill Frankel Hauser

Early Learning Skill-Builders
Colors, Shapes, Numbers & Letters
by Mary Tomczyk

Visit Our Website!

To see what's new at Williamson and learn more about specific books, visit our secure website at:

www.williamsonbooks.com
or www.Idealsbooks.com

---

3 Easy Ways to Order Books:

Please visit our secure website to place your order, or:

Toll-free phone orders: **1-800-586-2572**

Toll-free fax orders: **1-888-815-2759**

All major credit cards accepted (please include the number and expiration date).

Or, send a check with your order to:
Williamson Books
Orders, Dept B.O.B.
535 Metroplex Drive, Suite 250
Nashville, TN 37211

For large volume or retail orders, please call Lee Ann Bretz at
1-800-586-2572
Catalog request: mail, phone, or fax above numbers.

Please add **$4.00** for postage for one book plus **$1.00** for each additional book. Satisfaction is guaranteed or full refund without questions or quibbles.

Prices may be slightly higher when purchased in Canada.